THE MEETING OF LOVE AND KNOWLEDGE

Perennial Wisdom

WORLD PERSPECTIVES

Volumes already published

WORLD PERSPECTIVES . *Volume Fifteen*

Planned and Edited by RUTH NANDA ANSHEN

THE MEETING OF
LOVE AND KNOWLEDGE
Perennial Wisdom

BY MARTIN C. D'ARCY, S.J.

New York
HARPER & BROTHERS PUBLISHERS

50098

Contents

Contents

World Perspectives

IT IS the thesis of *World Perspectives* that man is in the process of developing a new consciousness which, in spite of his apparent spiritual and moral captivity, can eventually lift the human race above and beyond the fear, ignorance, brutality and isolation which beset it today. It is to this nascent consciousness, to this concept of man born out of a universe perceived through a fresh vision of reality, that *World Perspectives* is dedicated.

Only those spiritual and intellectual leaders of our epoch who have a paternity in this extension of man's horizons are invited to participate in this Series: those who are aware of the truth that beyond the divisiveness among men there exists a primordial unitive power since we are all bound together by a common humanity more fundamental than any unity of dogma; those who recognize that the centrifugal force which has scattered and atomized mankind must be replaced by an integrating structure and process capable of bestowing meaning and purpose on existence; those who realize that science itself, when not inhibited by the limitations of its own methodology, when chastened and humbled, commits man to an indeterminate range of yet undreamed consequences that may flow from it.

This Series endeavors to point to a reality of which scientific theory has revealed only one aspect. It is the commitment to this reality that lends universal intent to a scientist's most original and solitary thought. By acknowledging this frankly we shall restore science to the great family of human aspirations by which men hope to fulfill themselves in the world community as thinking and sentient beings. For our problem is to discover a principle of differentiation and yet relationship lucid enough to justify and to purify scientific, philosophic and all other knowledge, both discursive and intuitive, by accepting their interdependence. This is the crisis in consciousness made articulate through the crisis in science. This is the new awakening. This is the *declaration of dependence*.

Each volume presents the thought and belief of its author and points to the way in which religion, philosophy, art, science, economics, politics and history may constitute that form of human activity which takes the fullest and most precise account of variousness, possibility, complexity and difficulty. Thus *World Perspectives* endeavors to define that ecumenical power of the mind and heart which enables man through his mysterious greatness to re-create his life.

This Series is committed to a re-examination of all those sides of human endeavor which the specialist was taught to believe he could safely leave aside. It interprets present and past events impinging on human life in our growing World Age and envisages what man may yet attain when summoned by an unbending inner necessity to the quest of what is most exalted in him. Its purpose is to offer new vistas in terms of world and human development while refusing to betray the intimate correlation between universality and individuality, dynamics and form, freedom and destiny. Each author deals with the increasing realization that spirit and nature are not separate and apart; that intuition and reason must regain their importance as the means of perceiving and fusing inner being with outer reality.

World Perspectives endeavors to show that the conception of wholeness, unity, organism is a higher and more concrete conception than that of matter and energy. Thus an enlarged meaning of life, of biology, not as it is revealed in the test tube of the laboratory but as it is experienced within the organism of life itself, is attempted in this Series. For the principle of life consists in the tension which connects spirit with the realm of matter. The element of life is dominant in the very texture of nature, thus rendering life, biology, a trans-empirical science. The laws of life have their origin beyond their mere physical manifestations and compel us to consider their spiritual source. In fact, the widening of the conceptual framework has not only served to restore order within the respective branches of knowledge, but has also disclosed analogies in man's position regarding the analysis and synthesis of experience in apparently separated domains of knowledge suggesting the possibility of an ever more embracing objective description of the meaning of life.

Knowledge, it is shown in these books, no longer consists in a manipulation of man and nature as opposite forces, nor in the reduction of data to mere statistical order, to reductionist dogmatism, but is a means of liberating mankind from the destructive power of fear, pointing the way toward the goal of the rehabilitation of the human will and the rebirth of faith and confidence in the human person. The works published also endeavor to reveal that the cry for patterns, systems, and authorities is growing less insistent as the desire grows stronger in both East and West for the recovery of a dignity, integrity and self-realization which are the inalienable rights of man who may now guide change by means of conscious purpose in the light of rational experience.

Other vital questions explored relate to problems of international understanding as well as to problems dealing with prejudice and the resultant tensions and antagonisms. The growing perception and responsibility of our World Age point to the new reality that the individual person and the collective person supplement and integrate each other; that the thrall of totalitarianism of both left and right has been shaken in the universal desire to recapture the authority of truth and human totality. Mankind can finally place its trust not in a proletarian authoritarianism, not in a secularized humanism, both of which have betrayed the spiritual property right of history, but in a sacramental brotherhood and in the unity of knowledge. This new consciousness has created a widening of human horizons beyond every parochialism, and a revolution in human thought comparable to the basic assumption, among the ancient Greeks, of the sovereignty of reason; corresponding to the great effulgence of the moral conscience articulated by the Hebrew prophets; analogous to the fundamental assertions of Christianity; or to the beginning of a new scientific era, the era of the science of dynamics, the experimental foundations of which were laid by Galileo in the Renaissance.

An important effort of this Series is to re-examine the contradictory meanings and applications which are given today to such terms as democracy, freedom, justice, love, peace, brotherhood and God. The purpose of such inquiries is to clear the way for the foundation of a genuine *world* history not in terms of nation or race or culture but in terms of man in relation to God, to himself, his fellow man and the universe, that reach beyond immediate self-interest. For the meaning of the World Age consists in respecting man's hopes and dreams which lead to a deeper understanding of the basic values of all peoples.

World Perspectives is planned to gain insight into the meaning of man, who not only is determined by history but who also determines history. History is to be understood as concerned not only with the life of man on this planet but as including also such cosmic influences as interpenetrate our human world. This generation is discovering that history does not conform to the social optimism of modern civilization and that the organization of human communities and the establishment of freedom and peace are not only intellectual achievements but spiritual and moral achievements as well, demanding a cherishing of the wholeness of human personality, the "unmediated wholeness of feeling and thought," and constituting a never-ending challenge to man, emerging from the abyss of meaninglessness and suffering, to be renewed and replenished in the totality of his life.

Justice itself, which has been "in a state of pilgrimage and crucifixion" and now is being slowly liberated from the grip of social and political demonologies in the East as well as in the West, begins to question its own premises. The modern revolutionary movements which have challenged the sacred institutions of society by protecting social injustice in the name of social justice are examined and re-evaluated.

In the light of this, we have no choice but to admit that the *un*freedom against which freedom is measured must be retained with it, namely, that the aspect of truth out of which the night view appears to emerge, the darkness of our time, is as little abandonable as is man's subjective advance. Thus the two sources of man's consciousness are inseparable, not as dead but as living and complementary, an aspect of that "principle of complementarity" through which Niels Bohr has sought to unite the quantum and the wave, both of which constitute the very fabric of life's radiant energy.

There is in mankind today a counterforce to the sterility and danger of a quantitative, anonymous mass culture, a new, if sometimes imperceptible, spiritual sense of convergence toward world unity on the basis of the sacredness of each human person and respect for the plurality of cultures. There is a growing awareness that equality may not be evaluated in mere numerical terms but is proportionate and analogical in its reality. For when equality is equated with interchangeability, individuality is negated and the human person extinguished.

We stand at the brink of an age of the world in which human life presses forward to actualize new forms. The false separation of man and nature, of time and space, of freedom and security, is acknowledged and we are faced with a new vision of man in his organic unity and of history offering a richness and diversity of quality and majesty of scope hitherto unprecedented. In relating the accumulated wisdom of man's spirit to the new reality of the World Age, in articulating its thought and belief, *World Perspectives* seeks to encourage a renaissance of hope in society and of pride in man's decision as to what his destiny will be.

World Perspectives is committed to the recognition that

all great changes are preceded by a vigorous intellectual re-evaluation and reorganization. Our authors are aware that the sin of hubris may be avoided by showing that the creative process itself is not a free activity if by free we mean arbitrary, or unrelated to cosmic law. For the creative process in the human mind, the developmental processes in organic nature and the basic laws of the inorganic realm may be but varied expressions of a universal formative process. Thus *World Perspectives* hopes to show that although the present apocalyptic period is one of exceptional tensions, there is also at work an exceptional movement toward a compensating unity which refuses to violate the ultimate moral power at work in the universe, that very power upon which all human effort must at last depend. In this way we may come to understand that there exists an inherent independence of spiritual and mental growth which though conditioned by circumstances is never determined by circumstances. In this way the great plethora of human knowledge may be correlated with an insight into the nature of human nature by being attuned to the wide and deep range of human thought and human experience.

In spite of the infinite obligation of men and in spite of their finite power, in spite of the intransigence of nationalisms, and in spite of the homelessness of moral passions rendered ineffectual by the scientific outlook, beneath the apparent turmoil and upheaval of the present, and out of the transformations of this dynamic period with the unfolding of a world consciousness, the purpose of *World Perspectives* is to help quicken the "unshaken heart of well-rounded truth" and interpret the significant elements of the World Age now taking shape out of the core of that undimmed continuity of the creative process which restores man to mankind while deepening and enhancing his communion with the universe.

RUTH NANDA ANSHEN

New York, 1957

Introduction

THIS book owes its conception indirectly to a correspondence with the late Dr. Ananda K. Coomaraswamy. He wrote to me, after reading a book I had written on love, protesting against my interpretation of words like *mind* and *gnostic* and *wisdom*. He blamed me for betraying a great tradition current in both East and West, what, in fact, he considered to be the perennial wisdom. The ensuing discussion led me, not to change my own view, but to consider more closely this so-called "perennial wisdom." What its claims are will be found in the pages of this book, and as Mr. Aldous Huxley has taken up its cause and stated it as clearly as possible in *The Perennial Philosophy* and in his Introduction to the Mentor Book, *The Song of God: Bhagavad-Gita,* I have used these constantly for reference. Any attempt to bring East and West closer together must be welcome, and this is what the "perennial philosophy" aims to do. Its exponents, no doubt, hope that, if spiritual ideals can be shown to have a "highest common factor," the many competing civilizations may come to enjoy the peace of a common culture. As the reader will discover, I am in sympathy with the attempt to find an ideal acceptable to all, but I do not think that the perennial philosophy envisaged by Coomaraswamy, Aldous Huxley and others is the authentic version for which we should be looking. Like many international conferences which come to no conclusion, the entente proposed by these thinkers may lead the way to something better. What is being attempted on the economic and political level should have its counterpart on the philosophic and spiritual.

The subject matter of this book lends itself to generalizations and to the use of personified abstractions. Modern logicians, with some reason, frown on language of this sort *; but in a short book a tradition which has its justification in Scripture and has been followed by mystics, contemplatives and spiritual writers in East and West cannot be abandoned. The logician has a duty to unpack the meaning of a word or a sentence. Those whose purpose is not primarily the analysis of words and sentences need not be so scrupulous. Like the courteous professor who never finished a sentence for fear of insulting the intelligence of his hearers, writers can use a form of syncopation and rely on the good sense of the reader. It is no more inaccurate, for instance, to write, "Thee, Wisdom, have I loved," than to repeat, "Necessity is the mother of invention."

"If Socrates were a donkey, would he be wise?" is a conundrum logicians play with. It may well be asked whether one who is unwise should dare to write on the subject of wisdom. "Who paints a figure, if he cannot be it, cannot draw it," says Dante; and the writer of Ecclesiasticus gives the warning: "Seek not the things that are too high for thee." I am only too aware of the relevance of these warnings, and must take refuge in another saying from Ecclesiasticus: "If thou see a man of understanding, go to him early in the morning, and let thy foot wear the step of his doors." By conversing with the wise

---

* For a directive on the correct use of such language Mr. P. T. Geach's *Form and Existence* (Papers of the Aristotelian Society, 1955) may be consulted.

and reading their works, I hope that I have learned to write about them without folly. There is a point in the saying that a cat can look at a king.

A Catholic writing on the spiritual and contemplative life is all the time aware of the distinction between grace and nature. The promoters of a perennial wisdom discussed in the following pages do not accept this distinction. It is part of their argument that pagan and Christian sages have the same experience, and, despite differences of culture and creed, are clients of the same wisdom. For this reason I begin on their ground and move through the wisdom as expressed in various faiths and philosophies to a conclusion drawn, I hope, from the evidence.

MARTIN C. D'ARCY

THE MEETING OF LOVE AND KNOWLEDGE

Perennial Wisdom

I.

Homo Sapiens

ZOOLOGISTS describe man as the highest of the mammals and give him the name of Homo sapiens. The attribute has a richer significance than that primarily intended by these scientists. They restrict themselves to their subject matter and are content to mark the differences in bone formation and brain, the capacity of, for example, Neanderthal man and Pekin man and those skulls which have all the characteristics of historic man. But the word *sapiens,* if conveniently applied to some primitive bones, is also the proper description of man at his highest. The desire for wisdom has been the lever raising man from barbarism to the highest forms of civilization, and the prime mover behind the outstanding works of mankind in language, mathematics, the arts, science, philosophy and religion. By reason of its presence we can trace an affinity between the men in the caves of Altamira and Lascaux and a Plato or a Newton.

For a long time the inestimable value of wisdom has been recognized. It was set apart from all other forms of learning and knowledge, and its virtue was acclaimed in the religious literature of the East, in the Bible and in the supreme philosophical works of Greece. The saving grace of old age was felt to lie in the enjoyment of wisdom. Although the body grew feeble the spirit of man continued to develop, and out of its experience gained what far more than compensated for the wasting of physical strength. "Woe to the land that has young blood on the throne," unless it be cooled by the counsel of the old. In story and in art the sage is represented as gray-bearded and far-seeing and as the messenger of the gods or of God. Like Saul with Samuel, rulers rejected their guidance and admonitions only at their peril. As wise they were credited with having had access to the Source of all power and knowledge. They had conversed with God, and as the ancients thought that no one could see God with mortal eyes—or perhaps to symbolize that the eyes must be "shelled with double dark to find the uncreated light," they were said to be blind. Besides these renowned sages there were the simple and the true servants of their work who were regarded as wise in their degree, lawgivers and artists and craftsmen, sailors and workers in the field. This tradition has continued and to this day the advice of high and humble men and women in every profession and grade of life is sought because they have absorbed the lessons of nature and human life. From all of this it appears that wisdom in times past has been associated with philosophy—as is natural—and religion, with a due respect to the experience of age; nevertheless it is to some extent independent of professions and arts and learning, and it does not follow that because one happens to be a scientist or philosopher one is accordingly wise.

In Greco-Roman philosophy a distinction was made between speculative wisdom and practical wisdom, and this distinction was carried on by the medieval scholastics. Practical wisdom was given pride of place among the moral virtues, going under the name of Prudence—a name which has now unfortunately become almost synonymous with shrewdness and caution. In the book of Proverbs wisdom says of itself: "To shrewdness I am a near neighbor," but it goes on to explain: "And I occupy myself with deep designs." In the old and proper sense Prudence has "deep designs" because it acts with deliberation, looks before and after, judges from a mellow experience and from a standpoint which is ultimate and universal. It sorts out the relevant from the irrelevant and because of a right appraisal of the end in view it lights upon the means which are properly proportioned to it. After a while it can act almost instinctively; a habit is formed by love and practice combined, making, for instance, the lover of justice almost invariably fair and keen-sighted in his judgments. We have no word now which is quite adequate for the old meaning, and so we have to find paraphrases such as "good judgment" or "deep discernment." How highly it was once esteemed can be read in the book of Proverbs: "Good counsel is mine, and honourable dealing. . . . Through me kings learn how to reign, lawgivers how to lay down just decrees; through me chieftains and magistrates exercise their power aright. . . . The man who wins me, wins life, drinks deep of the Lord's favour; who fails, fails at his own bitter cost; to be my enemy is to be in love with death."

These words from the Bible assume an intimate connection of prudence and wisdom with religion, and the same assumption is made in other literatures. The functions of king, high priest and sage were inseparable, and this was natural in a world which believed in a divine source of all wisdom and power, from which was derived all human authority. In England learning was for many centuries a clerical preserve and ecclesiastics held the position of the Lord Chancellor and were "keepers of the king's conscience." The gradual devolution of knowledge into separate departments and the separation of church and state may well have had something to do with the downfall of the hierarchy of the sciences and of the old established supremacy of wisdom at the top. Certainly in the West, as contrasted with the East, interest in and love of wisdom for its own sake declined. Trade, too, and industry turned men's minds to the active life. What has also counted is the paramount confidence in reason, where by reason is meant the discursive reason as exhibited in the new scientific methods adopted. Reason came to be regarded as the one worth-while activity of man, in fact the only intellectual activity. Poetry and religion were allowed as extracurricular exercises; the imaginative, the subconscious and the mystical were treated as interlopers. As a result the philosopher has tended to become a scholar and a logician. Ideas are separated from their human entanglements and treated in a vacuum. They are examined one by one under the searchlight of reason and passed if they emerge as reasonable and consistent. All that does not fall under this searchlight is dismissed as irrational or as irrelevant. With philosophers so detached and with all engaged on their separate business wisdom has suffered. The impoverishment is only now being realized. "You may throw nature out with a fork, but it always returns," and at times it returns in frightening forms. The dehumanized logic of Hegel drove Kierkegaard into rebellion. Marx, too, revolted, and though he believed his dialectic could stand firm against any rational criticism, he despised the theorists and overturned reason. Schopenhauer and Nietzsche and Bergson and others were malcontents, but the significance of their protests has only recently been fully realized. Now nature is taking its revenge. The existentialists have captured a large public, and the language of the unconscious and of myth is on everyone's lips. Human reason unsupported by its other powers and by religion has been put on the defensive, and large numbers have turned away from the rationalists to consult Sartre and Gabriel Marcel and to discuss the primordial images of Jung and the wisdom contained in the myth. In the high cultures of the past wisdom was compact of thought, love and imagination, and kept art under the protection of mind, while art and poetry supplied thought with figures and analogies. The abstractions also of philosophy came to life in the creeds and experiences of religion. Rationalism relying on its own resources, and especially when divorced from religion, grew arid, a wasteland no longer watered by human experience. It became an affair of coteries, and the discipline of philosophy turned into a school for acute analyses and endless discussion of intellectual puzzles—in fact, an Areopagus of the sophisticated.

This picture is very different from that of the past, whether pagan or Christian. The story is told in the Chronicle of St. Gall of two Irish monks who set sail in a boat and arrived on the shores of France. They walked to a market town, and on being asked what they had brought to market, they answered: "Wisdom; nothing but wisdom!" Their intention, they said, was not to sell it, but to give it free to anyone who might care for it; in return they asked for nothing but shelter and food.

Charlemagne heard of them, and was so impressed and eager for their wares that he sent messengers to them and persuaded them to come and teach him and his court. The story, so Gilson informs us, is no mere legend, for Alcuin of York did accept an invitation from Charlemagne and go to his court, there to teach the beginning of that wisdom, which spread to Chartres and the University of Paris. Young and old were, indeed, at the time thirsting for knowledge, as the conquistadors for gold, and the youth flocked from one place to another on hearing of a great teacher, to listen to the voice of an Abelard or sit on the straw in the cold halls where Siger de Brabant or St. Thomas Aquinas lectured on wisdom and the manner of attaining it. That this is no exaggeration is proved by the fact that St. Thomas opens his course of teaching with the praise of wisdom and says of it that "of all human pursuits, that of wisdom is the most perfect, the most sublime, the most profitable, the most delightful." He had in mind the great passages from the Bible, and it was in the atmosphere of the Biblical ideal of wisdom that students listened and doctors taught. In an age of faith, and at a time when a new world was opening out words such as the following came as an irresistible ideal and summons. "The Lord made me his when first he went about his work, at the birth of time, before his creation began. . . . I was there when he enclosed the sea within its confines, forbidding the waters to transgress their assigned limits, when he poised the foundations of the world. I was at his side, a master workman, my delight increasing with each day, as I made play before him all the while; made play in this world of dust, with the sons of Adam for my playfellows. Listen to me, then, you that are my sons, that follow, to your happiness, in the paths I show you; listen to the teaching that will make you wise, instead of turning away from it."

The documents of the Near and Far East testify to the same passion for wisdom, though, as might be expected, the word has subtly different connotations. Tao is the proper way to go, the way of nature and universal law, and, as Lao-tsu said: "Whose offspring it may be, I do not know; it is like a preface to God." Both in Hindu and Buddhist teaching wisdom is the way to union with the highest, the way of deliverance from the deceptions of this world. There is no need to do more than call attention to the immense influence of Plato and the Neo-Platonists; as Plato suggests, true knowledge is imaged in the golden earring with a siren playing the lyre, the symbol of im-mortality and of union with the godhead. The writings of Nicholas Berdyaev and other Russian exiles have reminded us of the supreme reverence paid to sophia in the Orthodox Church, a reverence visibly manifested in the great Basilica of Constantinople. The West has moved away from this tradition and is now distrustful of speculative wisdom. I have already suggested reasons for this change, the gradual secularization of knowledge, the age of reason and the multiplication of sciences, each complete within its own domain and committed to a purely empirical approach. The rule of setting limits and re-garding all outside as irrelevant has spread to other disciplines and notably to literary criticism. The change is well illustrated by the difference of attitude of two such writers as Santayana and Mr. I. A. Richards, whose lives overlap. Santayana car-ries on the teaching of Aristotle that poetry is nearer philosophy and more worth while than history. Hence in reading Dante what appeals to him is the poet's wisdom. The Greek theoria reached in him, he says, its consummation. Philosophy loses its abstract quality and becomes embodied in a vision—the past and the present, the personal and the traditional are fused; and "the fancy is not empty or arbitrary; it is serious, fed on the study of real things. It adopts their tendency and divines their true destiny. The art is an imitation or rehearsal of nature, an anticipation of fate. For this reason curious details of science or history enter as a matter of course into his verse," and therefore the landscape becomes a semblance of the divine intention. The whole world becomes his canvas, and seen there, "that world becomes complete, clear, beautiful and tragic. It is vivid and truthful in its detail, sublime in its march and its harmony." Mr. Richards, on the other hand, is impatient of this philosophizing and has argued that belief in the presuppositions and content of the *Divine Comedy* is irrelevant to a proper appreciation of it, and he has reduced the judgment of value to a harmonization of impulses. Even Mr. T. S. Eliot, in whose own poetry many have caught glimpses of a past and present wisdom, warns us that "in the dogmatic or lazy mind comparison is supplied by judgment, analysis replaced by appreciation. Judgment and appreciation are merely tolerable avocations, no part of the critic's serious business."

No doubt Mr. Eliot had in mind those bad critics who instead of starting from the ground indulge in airy generalities; no doubt, too, that much of the new criticism is salutary. But in so far as it represents the view that the large issues over which the ancients pored are waste of time, it is an act of defiance of the old wisdom and the old tradition. "The science of agriculture and a due reverence for the gods were not opposed for Virgil; they united to form one theme; and even the

materialist Lucretius sees behind his jarring atoms the beneficent power of alma Venus, the mother of his people, delight
of gods and men." * The stores and the market places of the
great cities are full of the amenities of life, showing how the
minds of inventors, engineers and editors are engaged in practical improvements to living. The monks would look strange
in such surroundings with their offer to provide wisdom gra-
tuitously. At a recent meeting in New York concerned with a
cultural interchange between the English-speaking countries
and Japan, one member remarked: "We have obviously much
to give the Japanese, but what have the Japanese to give in
return?" "You forget," replied another member, "that we have
lost something still preserved in the East, the respect for the
sage." The answer found its mark, because those present were
conscious of a dearth and felt vaguely perhaps what is made
explicit in the following words. "The empirical intelligence of
modern Western man has been formed by a bare three hundred years of organized scientific speculation; he lives by his
achievements; without them he would perish. But they have
very little to do with the spiritual and imaginative aliment of
his ancestors, which still, inevitably, form the soil and ground-
work of his mind. So that we all have the powerful external
forces that move matter in space and make the organization
of modern society possible, existing in dissociation from the
emotional, imaginative and spiritual foundations of man's
mind." † Japan is tempted to imitate the industrial civilization of the West and leave the dead sages to bury their dead.

* Mr. Graham Hough in the *Twentieth Century,* February, 1955, pp.
109–110.
† *Ibid.,* p. 110.

But it still has the memory of men who trained themselves by silence and solitude and reading and meditation and so came to a knowledge superior to that of the multitudes engrossed in fighting and bargaining. Its history is alive with names of men who gathered disciples round them, formed a school and communicated a way of wisdom, Honen and Shinran and Eisai, who brought Zen Buddism from China, and Nichiren, who, despite his tetchiness, inspired reverence and gained a position to which there is no equivalent now in England or America. Japan learned from China and Chinese Buddhism came from India. The wise man fitted into those societies, whereas he seems out of place in a society which will not go behind a common or "horse" sense.

Were there no other evidence of dissatisfaction than the contempt into which the name *bourgeois* has fallen, that in itself would be enough to point to a radical change in modern, Western society. But in fact the heart-searching and soul-seeking are so prevalent as to be overdone. The burden of the song is that we have lost something vital and it must be recovered. Claimants to wisdom are being examined, and there are many, occultism, psychological healing, humanitarian Communism, a perennial philosophy and poetry. Poets have for a long time gone hand in hand with the seers, but in more recent days, as Mr. Stephen Spender complains, many have turned to a private universe of their own, while others have consorted with the magic seers. Yeats, for instance, with his love for the sleeping beauty of Ireland and its ancestral myths, felt that the poet must be a sage. As he wrote to the Lady Elizabeth Pelham: "It seems to me that I have found what I wanted. . . . When I try to put it into a phrase I say, 'man can embody truth but he cannot know it.' The abstract is not life and everywhere draws out its contradiction. You can refute Hegel but not the Saint or the Song of Sixpence." But the truth as he came to hold it was mixed with the occult, and his sight was troubled with the great images "out of the spiritus mundi." No wonder he admired Goethe's *Wilhelm Meister* as "the wisest of all books." Dr. Faustus is the symbol of those who despair because "the new locus is never hidden inside the old one where Reason could rout it out," and they have hope that it "is guarded in distant mountains where Imagination could explore it." When wisdom is clouded in the daytime we wait to worship it in the moonshine. To judge from Scripture the quest for a forbidden knowledge began early, and there are to be found strange rites and initiations mingled in most of the great religious known to history. There is black magic and white magic, there are witch doctors and monk sorcerers, there are alchemists and followers of Trismegistus. In the closed universe of the last century new cults propagating a hidden and higher wisdom have proliferated. Many of these belong rather to the category of occultism than wisdom; but there is one cult—it cannot be called new except in the form in which it appears— which contains a hidden and superior knowledge and claims to be the perennial wisdom. It is the challenge of this wisdom I wish to meet.

Mr. Aldous Huxley in a book which he has entitled *The Perennial Philosophy,* has given us the clearest exposition of this new religious philosophy which has been gaining ground ever since part of the religious literature of the East has been translated and publicized. Dean Inge and other Christian writers have already used the title "perennial wisdom" for a supposed highest common factor in the writings of Western philosophers. In their view Europe inherited from the Bible, from Greece and from Rome a set of ideas, which fusing together have become the unfailing support and stimulus of Western civilization. The truths contained in them are the life blood of man. The spiritual riches, however, revealed in other cultures, especially those with a background of mystical religion, has persuaded a number of thinkers from different countries to widen the terms of reference. They are engaged on a task not wholly unlike that undertaken at the beginning of the twentieth century. Comparative religion was then in its heyday, and scholars were busy finding likenesses in the rites, stories and doctrines of the various religions and tracing them all to one natural origin. This was a search for the lowest common denominator. Mr. Aldous Huxley and René Guénon and Frithjof and the distinguished Indian scholar Coomaraswamy and others are likewise interested in comparing the various religions, but their purposes are different. They do not look first to the stories and practices; the rites and symbols and myths may differ; nevertheless they may point in the same direction; and it is with the highest common factor, with the ideals which are expressed, that they are concerned. They take a fact such as the prevalence of some center in the countries where a religion is practiced. This center is held sacred as the center of the universe, the meeting place of heaven and earth, the Greek *omphalos,* the Jewish Tabor or Mount Gerizim, the Indian Mount Meru and the mountain of Zinnalo. The significance of these centers is that they show the perennial belief in a distinction between a higher region of life and the one in which man is now placed; the higher region is in heaven, but there is a meeting place in the center, which is therefore held as sacred. They point to this common belief and to others as insights into the destiny of man. They rely, too, on what is called the sense of the numinous, an expression invented by Rudolf Otto to convey the peculiar quality of all genuine religious experience, a quality which separates it off from moral or aesthetic reactions, and is aroused by the presence of the "holy." In its presence man is overwhelmed by the sense of his nothingness, and yet is drawn beyond himself toward this infinite being or reality. Guénon is convinced that this sense of the numinous is a real and genuine phenomenon and present in the creation of religious symbolism and ritual. Properly understood, therefore, they bespeak, amid all the various disguises and aberrations of the different faiths, one universal and single tendency and ideal, that religious wisdom, in fact, which is the key and finale of all great civilizations and religions.

This tradition is a metaphysical one embedded in religion. What in a primitive or adolescent society flowers in myth and symbol and ritual takes on a metaphysical countenance when thought and reflection develop. The significance of the symbols and the ritual is realized as pointing to a distinction of two worlds, a world apart which must be sought by a special gnosis, and the world of appearance and time in which man's days are passed. A most striking example of this development is to be found in India in the rise of the Upanishads and what is known as the Vedanta, but it is also seen in the maturity of the Greek, Egyptian, Babylonian and Chinese cultures. In some of these cultures a sublimated mythology predominates, in others the mystical element. In each the soul is liberated from darkness into light, from the material into the spiritual. In Gnosticism, for instance, the soul escapes from necessity, from the pressure of the stars and planets, the signs of the zodiac and from all the demonic powers. Instead of subjugation, the soul, as a Coptic Gnostic treatise expresses it, rises above all these powers: "And you shall possess aeons and worlds and heavens, so that the intelligible spirits come and they dwell in them. And you shall be deified, and you shall know that you came forth from God, and you shall see that he is God within you; and he shall dwell in your aeon." Mythology is certainly not absent from the Hindu religions, but in the Upanishads it is metaphysics which takes the principal part, and this metaphysics, so the advocates of the perennial wisdom claim, is an expression of what lies behind, and in, all religion. The reason why they make this claim is this: this metaphysic teaches that in its highest reaches the self attains to complete unity with the object of its thought. The distinctions which we make in everyday life of subject and an objective world over against us are overcome. Now in this present world of appearances and of illusion we think of ourselves as individuals, separate atoms, so to speak, touching and glancing off one another. We have to die to this self, and by a process of prayer and concentration pass into a different condition, which discards images and concepts and discursive thought, loses count of time and space, and finally realizes that the self belongs to the whole and is utterly at one with it. This is the point where true metaphysics and mysticism meet in the ineffable experience, which has to be described in terms of intuition or identity, though in fact no words can do it justice.

This wisdom is, therefore, a kind of gnosis, and it stipulates that there are degrees of knowledge, that ordinary knowledge is an instrument which is finally to be superseded by a still higher state. The first degree is one of make-believe, the candlelight which will be unnecessary when the sun shines. The world of time and place and separate individual life is one of illusion relatively to that which is fully real. Our ignorance magnifies the importance of what we feel and see around us. "Knowledge," as Professor Radhakrishnan tells us, "is concealed in ignorance and when the latter is removed the former manifests itself. What we are that we behold, and what we behold that we are. Our thought, our life and our being are uplifted in simplicity and we are made one with truth." The lesson which we are to learn from this is that man must seek for ultimate truth and not rest in his earth-bound experience. Evidence is now everywhere at hand and its testimony is so converging among the great religions of the world that no one should dare to doubt the presence of this perennial wisdom. Guénon and Schuon and Aldous Huxley are all insistent on this, and so they look to a way of life which is one of uncompromising denial of this world's values. Such values stand in the way of the mystical or intuitive knowledge which can be attained. Some of them hold, also, that what is so unmistakable in the Eastern religions and also in the loftier cults of the Near East is recognizable in Christianity, though its history has been so ambiguous. Guénon with his flair for metaphysics almost despairs of the West because of its preoccupation with material welfare and the social and political liberties of the individual. Its values seem to him pragmatic, and the fact, in his eyes, that Protestantism has so often viewed mysticism askance and dispensed with the intellectual element in its faith makes it for him a lost cause. Alone in the Catholic medieval metaphysics can he find any contact with the superior wisdom he admires. A scholastic philosopher does keep some continuity with the knowledge of the East and is in a position to understand it. Schuon, on the other hand, regards the Catholic faith as the enemy of knowledge. In this matter he probably is confusing the caution which the Catholic Church has shown toward certain scientific hypotheses with its general attitude to speculation. If he had argued that the Catholic Church, by preferring Aristotle to Plato, had cut its connection with Eastern thought, he would have made a point—not, however, a valid one in the opinion of many. The Platonic influence, so experts are now inclined to believe, is stronger than was once supposed in the system of, for example, St. Thomas Aquinas. It is certainly present in the field of mysticism because the writings of Denys the Areopagite, owing to their supposed apostolic origin, were in great favor. Plato, without question, belongs to the tradition which Guénon and Schuon have in mind, and this tradition continues through the Neo-Platonists to St. Augustine, and from him down through the Christian centuries. Nor is Aristotle himself outside this same tradition. In more than one place he gives a careful description of what he means by wisdom, and he finds room for an intuitive form of knowledge which is higher than discursive reasoning. His theory of knowledge, indeed, has affinities with the Indian and Platonic ideal. St. Thomas adopted it and in its terms marked out the varying degrees of union with God which are possible for a human being.

In the perennial philosophy as presented by Guénon man reaches up to an intuitive knowledge of the divine, and in the final stage is made one with the Godhead. Man loses his identity, and becomes instead of a finite, separate and existing being truly one in essence with what is infinite and perfect.

This does not strike us at first as impossible or unintelligible, because lovers all the world over use the same kind of language. In the well-known Persian story the lover comes to the house of the beloved and knocks. When asked who is there, he answers: "It is I." The beloved replies: "There is no room for you and me." He tries vainly again and again. Finally when asked the same question, he answers: "It is Thou," and the door opens. Profane love has the same language as divine:

> So they lov'd, as love in twain
> Had the essence but in one;
> Two distincts, division none,
> Number there in love was slain.

But be it noted, there are "two distincts"; the union here is of persons and persons do not fuse like thoughts. Guénon uses the language of mind with mind, and this ignores the fact that it is a subject who thinks and not a mind. But even where mind is united with an object or another mind Aristotle is a useful pedagogue, and St. Thomas managed to avoid the extreme position of Guénon by adapting the Aristotelian theory to explain all forms of knowing from the lowest to the highest. Knowing is an activity, he says, and analogous to other living activities. In eating, for instance, we take what is not ourselves and make it our own; the honeyed cake after consumption becomes part of our bodily life. Analogously, when we are thinking of honey and know what it is, the idea of it which has been grasped by the mind is indistinguishable from the actual honey. The honey-as-thought-of is ours; it is a piece of knowledge which we have acquired, and at the same time it is one and the same as the actual honey, except that the actual honey is in no way affected by this appropriation of it by the mind. It remains existing there in the comb, the while it now also exists in our minds. Hence the saying of Aristotle, that "the intelligible in act and the intellect in act are one and the same save for the mode of existence"; in other words, anything which is intelligible when it is actually understood is the same as the fruit of the mind when it understands it. In everyday experience we may have a vivid image of a friend. This is in the sensible order. In the intellectual order, if we understood him fully, then we should be entirely one with him, and yet distinct. So far from losing our identity, in fact, if this account of knowledge be acceptable, we should grow in knowledge and be more ourselves, the closer the union with another. The Catholic theologians applied this theory of knowledge when faced with the mystery of God's union with the soul. They took the text of Scripture, "in thy light we shall see light," and the other promise that "we shall be like to Him, for we shall see Him as He is in Himself" as their clue. Since no human idea, however exalted, could be a true and adequate likeness or replica of the infinite being of God, and since we are destined, by grace, to see and enjoy Him, it must be, they argued, that God Himself took the place of the human representation and filled the soul with His presence. As St. Francis of Sales exclaimed: "What happiness for the human mind to be united for ever to its sovereign object, receiving not an idea or representation, but the very essence of His divine truth and majesty."

This experience was regarded as the supreme case of *intuition* by these thinkers. All the writers on perennial knowledge in the East and West use this word *intuition* as offering an explanation of what they mean. It is not, however, too easy to understand, especially as in ordinary converse we use it loosely for whatever is swift and direct in knowledge. We speak of sense intuition, of having an intuition of what is wrong with a man, of the poets' and mathematicians' intuition which arrives at truths while the reason lags behind. Philosophers employ the word, for they can seldom do without it, but the sense in which they use it varies. It is applied to knowledge arrived at directly and immediately, and it is regarded as a form of knowing superior to that of ordinary thinking and reasoning, as belonging to a realm of knowledge with which the accepted methods of reasoning cannot cope. There must be, it is thought, an experience at the top level which will correspond with what happens at the lowest level. At the lowest level, namely that of sense experience, we seem to have a direct experience of color and sound, and we are inclined to think that we cannot be in error in seeing what we see. Where error comes in is in our interpretation of what we see. I cannot be mistaken in seeing blue, no matter whether it be proved to be an optical delusion or the result of fever. If asked how and why we can be so certain we may fall back on the self-evident, or argue that so direct is the experience it leaves no room for mistake. Because it is so immediate we give it the name of intuition. In all such experiences, however, it is not easy to be sure how much we see and how much we assume we see. For years philosophers have written about objects called sense data, though investigation and experiment show that we never see sense data by themselves; they occur in groups and constellations, and what we perceive are spaced and colored things. Moreover, these presentations always have incipient meanings for us, and we look at them with the help of memory and association. They do retain, however, a directness compared with objects about which we have to learn, and so the word *intuition* does not seem out of place. The objects we have to learn and think about are very different. We enter a world of abstractions, constructions, experiment and multiple observation, and the process of reasoning and making hypotheses and of circling round objects never comes to an end. So limited and artificial, indeed, does our rational knowledge of nature seem to be that the debate starts up again and again as to the authenticity of the knowledge so obtained. Philosophers and scientists are tempted in their dissatisfaction to declare that scientific knowledge is not of nature at all, that it is a pointer reading or an arbitrary, though consistent, system of symbols and determined by the machinery of our mind. The faith in science and philosophy, nevertheless, persists, and many are consoled by what seems to be a more direct apprehension and grasp of the nature of things. To such insights, glimpses and gleams of truth they give the name of "intuition," borrowing it from sensible experience and as a foretaste of what they would like to have. Such an intuition would be much richer than that of sensible experience. Knowledge is concerned with the how and the why, and so the intuitions of the wise man would comprise a manifold articulated into a whole so as to form a unity and a meaningful unity. The intuition grasps this unity and sees in it why and how all is held together. Moreover this intuition is of the mind and as what the mind possesses belongs to it, there would be no longer any barriers between the subject and the object. The immediacy of the knowledge should mean strictly that all intermediaries had been removed, so that the knower and the known would be one in a much more proper and complete sense than with sensible experience. This philosophical analysis it is which explains the high talk of the religious philosophers of the East and the mystics of every age, and it is to this kind of knowledge that the sage directs the disciple, leading him from the half truths, the abstractions, the fugitive gleams, the agglomeration of bits of knowledge to that wisdom which consists in an understanding of the meaning of all reality and an identification of himself with it.

In the wisdom as understood by Guénon and Coomaraswamy and others there are various grades; those upon "the path" are separated from the profane crowds who are content with common sense or empirical knowledge. This division runs through many of the great religions, like the division of day from night. There are the initiates and the guardians or masters of the mysteries, the bacchants who are rare compared with the wand bearers. From the importance given to the clergy and from the habit in the early Christian Church of keeping certain doctrines secret from the pagan—the so-called *disciplina arcani* —some have assumed that Christianity too has a similar division. But this would be a mistaken conclusion. There is no esoteric as contrasted with an exoteric doctrine, and all are called to the same spiritual perfection. The reserve of the early Church was due to its fear of the coarse-minded pagan misunderstanding such spiritual doctrines as the Eucharist, the partaking of the Body and Blood of Christ. The wisdom of the other religions, on the other hand, is almost always a form of gnosis, something secret and hidden, and it belongs to a chosen few. Even amongst the few there are degrees of initiation, as there are in jujitsu, and the rare masters hand on their technique and their counsels and sayings to disciples who create a school and a tradition. As in all such schools variations and rivalries abound; the one will advocate concentration with eyes open, the other that the eyes should be shut in the silence of concentration. Dr. Suzuki quotes the words of Hakuin on the relative merits of the Nembutsu and the koan exercise and of how the koan has the advantage in that it emphasizes "a strong spirit of inquiry." "Therefore it is said that the stronger the inquiring spirit, the greater the resulting satori, and that a sufficiently strong spirit of inquiry is sure to result in strong satori. Further, according to Fo-Kuo, the greatest fault with Zen devotees is the lack of an inquiring spirit over the koan. When their inquiring spirit reaches its highest point of fixation there is a moment of outburst." The difference here between the Nembutsu and the koan exercise is interesting in having a far-off likeness to a divergence among Christian directors on the subject of prayer. The Nembutsu, as Suzuki tells us, arose in the early days of Buddhism in India. In India and in China, as the religion became popular among the people, an elementary form of union with the Buddha was taught. This consisted in the recitation of the Buddha's name or of some extremely simple formula, and the disciple had to think of the Buddha while doing so. This form of prayer was to be accompanied by complete reliance on the Buddha. The Zen reformers criticized this form of prayer as mechanical; there should be more attention to the sense of what was being recited, and there should be more reliance upon the self—an echo in far Japan of British Pelagianism! As one of the Zen masters wrote: "The idea of the invocation is to know that the Buddha is no other than your own mind; but what is this mind? See into the *whence* of your thought which makes you utter the name of the Buddha;

where does it originate? But you must go even further than this and make inquiries as to the *who* of this person who wants to see into the whence of a thought. Is it mind, or Buddha, or matter? No, it is none of these, say the masters. What is it then?"

These questions of the Zen master do, indeed, bear on the nature and subject of wisdom.

II.

Wisdom and Mysticism

M. E.–A. PREYRE in his *The Freedom of Doubt* puts side by side the saying from the Chandogya Upanishad: "When a man being asleep, reposing and at perfect rest, sees not dreams, that is his Self . . . this is Brahman," and Miguel de Unamuno's: "Limitless Unconsciousness, which is our knowledge of God." Separated by centuries and by different cultures, these two writers, nevertheless, seem to express the same thought. Aldous Huxley would have it that no matter how differently worded the wisdom of the East and West may be, it is identical below the surface. Ananda Coomaraswamy maintains that this identity is reflected even in religious art: "A fundamental identity of European and Asiatic art, transcending all possible stylistic differences, and all possible distinction of themes." Asia, however, has not suffered from the distractions and deviations of the West; for it "has consistently and consciously acted in an awareness that the goal is only reached when the knower and the known, subject and object, are identified in one experience. In European religion the application of this doctrine has been a heresy. In India it has been a cardinal principle of devotion that to worship God one must become God" (*Introduction to the Art of Eastern Asia,* p. 13).

Coomaraswamy here distinguishes between the doctrine of identity and the application of it. He implies that whereas the application of it has been a heresy in Europe the doctrine itself is the orthodox tradition. This is a startling assertion. The Bible, which is the textbook of Western religion, contains no such doctrine, and almost every article in the Christian Creed implies an absolute distinction between God the creator and man the creature. In the Christian teaching the living God, creator of heaven and earth, freely raises man to a new status of union and possible happiness with Himself. Man still preserves his own identity, the while he is "bathed in the fall-gold mercies and breathes in the all-fire glances" of divine love. Moreover, in the Christian tradition final wisdom is not out of all relation with human knowledge. Our present light is, indeed, darkness in comparison with the splendor to come of the beatific vision; but there is no complete break between the one and the other. If, as Montaigne complains, our "self overweening" would "sift his divinities through our sieve," the humbled self, nevertheless, can become a receptacle of divine truth.

Such a theory must, according to Coomaraswamy, fall short of the truth. Nothing below identity will suffice, for, as he says, true wisdom is an "awareness that the goal is only reached when the knower and the known, subject and object, are identified in one experience." In the light of this all our human values and standards and thoughts must be judged as vain. What then is this identity? Some are content to call it inexpressible. Much nevertheless has been written about it, with the result too often of spreading darkness instead of light. "In the root divine wisdom is all-Brahman; in the stem she is all-Illusion; in the flower she is all-World; and in the fruit all-Liberation" (Tantra-Tatva). Zen texts tell us to be "serene in the oneness of things," and to abide "in the immovable serenity of non-assertion." In the Talavakara-Upanishad we are told that "he by whom it [Brahman] is not thought, by him it is thought; he by whom it is thought, knows it not." But any thought may be an obstacle—for "bidding farewell to any knowledge I am become one with the Great Pervader" (Kwang-tze, Book XXIII, Part III). The texts I have chosen —and they could be multiplied—have some reference in them to wisdom and knowledge, and the first effect on the mind is of incoherence. Let it be admitted that in their context they do serve to convey an experience which can be communicated only by a series of paradoxes. The art which does this successfully must be respected. But when we seek to learn from it more precisely what is the identity and what is the wisdom it deals with, this art disappoints, perhaps because we are asking more than it can give. It may be that the mystical experience should not be used to create a framework of philosophy on the nature of God and of the self and of the world. It is too subjective, too esoteric; it is unendorsed and without security. The mystics are like the poets who so disappointed Socrates; they say wonderful things about wisdom, but they cannot always tell us what it is. The Western outlook has been greatly influenced by the Greek philosophy, and in that philosophy wisdom has an important role and also its definition. Socrates sought for wisdom, and Plato and Aristotle pondered over it and bequeathed an interpretation of it, which St. Thomas and other medieval thinkers inserted into the Christian philosophy. St. Thomas recapitulates past thinking on the subject in these words: "Among other things which men conceive of the wise man, Aristotle reckons that it 'belongs to the wise man to direct things.' " Now the rule of all things is this, he says; that to find the value of things we should look to see what end they serve and judge them by their fittingness to that end. Among the arts, for instance, "the medical art rules and directs the art of the druggist, because health which is the object of medicine is the end of all drugs which are made up by the druggist's art. The same may be observed in the art of sailing in relation to the art of ship-building, and in the military art in relation to the equestrian art and all warlike appliances. These arts which govern others are called master arts, that is principal arts, for which reason their craftsmen are awarded the name of wise men. Since, however, these same craftsmen, through being occupied with the ends of certain singular things, do not attain to the universal end of all things they are called wise about this or that, in which sense it is said: 'as a wise architect, I have laid the foundation,' whereas the name of being wise simply is reserved to him alone whose consideration is about the end of the universe, which end is also the beginning of the universe: wherefore according to Aristotle, it belongs to the wise man to consider the highest causes."

Here is a description of the wise philosopher, but St. Thomas was also a theologian and a spiritual genius—and the "perennial wisdom" in the eyes of all its supporters is a religious philosophy. This then will be the wisdom which we must examine. The provisional divisions are obvious. One will be theological knowledge, another contemplation, and the third mystical experience. The same man may possess all these three forms of wisdom, and our first distinctions may prove to overlap or merge into each other. St. Thomas, for example, was a theologian, and according to his biographers also a contemplative and mystic. It is said that at the end of his short life he was caught up in such ecstasies of prayer that he declared his writings "to be but straw compared to what he now saw." Plotinus, again, was a great religious philosopher and enjoyed mystical experiences. Theoretically it is quite possible for a man to create a great system of theology and deserve the name of wise without being either a contemplative or mystic. The system stands there for inspection and judgment, no matter what kind of a person the author happened to be. In fact, however, the best-known writers, whether in the East or in Russia or nearer home have united in themselves a spiritual ardor with close-knit thought. They have, too, a very modest idea of themselves, for as St. Thomas remarks of Pythagoras: "When asked what he professed himself to be, Pythagoras was unlike his predecessors and would lay no claim to be a wise man, for to him that appeared presumptuous; he professed to be a philosopher, that is a lover of wisdom." Socrates, as is well known, also fought shy of the designation "wise," and came to the conclusion that the oracle's words about him could be true only in the sense that he knew his ignorance. St. Thomas is prepared to say that the theologian and the genuine metaphysician ought to be happier than others, for the "final joy of man consists in the superlative activity of his supreme power, namely the activity of mind engaged with incomparable truth. . . . Absolutely speaking, the first causes of things should possess the most and noblest meanings, for they are superlatively real and consequently the truest. Though these first causes of all other realities may appear less evident to us, the most complete happiness open to us in our present life really consists in considering them. The glimpse we catch is lovelier and more sublime than any understanding of lesser things." But I doubt if he is here thinking only of the dry essences with which the metaphysician tries to grapple. What was ultimate was to him alive and lovable, and he was always a religious contemplative. "Contemplation can be delightful both as a function and for its content. The activity is congenial to human nature and instinct, and especially when a man thereby holds a thing he loves. Thus seeing is enjoyable itself, and more so when it gazes on the form of the beloved." In other words his mind is fertilized by love, and what he means by wisdom is gazing "on the form of the beloved." That is why in the beginning of his greatest work he prefaces it with a passage which contains echoes throughout of the words of the Bible and sentences from the Book of Wisdom. As it is there written: "Wisdom is an infinite treasure to men; which they that use become the friends of God"; and it is the most delightful because wisdom's "conversation hath no bitterness, nor her company any tediousness, but joy and gladness."

The religious philosopher, faithful as he must always be to truth, is spurred by love or desire. This holds good both in the East and the West. I say "or desire" because Suzuki tells us that "alike in India, China, and Japan, satori has remained thoroughly impersonal, or rather highly intellectual." But there must be a wholehearted desire. Tu-feng Chi-shan, for instance, who lived in the latter half of the fifteenth century, told his pupils: "If you are determined to escape birth and death, a great believing heart is first of all to be awakened and great vows to be established. Let this be your prayer: So long as the koan I am holding this moment is not solved, so long as my own face which I have even prior to my birth is not seen, so long as the subtle deeds of transmigration are not destroyed, I made up my mind most resolutely not to abandon the koan given me for solution, not to keep myself away from wise teachers, and not to become a greedy pursuer of fame and wealth; and when these determinations are deliberately violated, may I fall back in the evil paths. Establishing this vow, keep a steady watch over your heart so that you will be a worthy recipient of a koan." Strong as the desire must be, the intellectual element in this education is not ignored. It is, however, subdued for the sake of the end in view. As Suzuki explains, the koan exercise is used to bring the pupil into a highly wrought state of consciousness, and so instead of the master allowing him to think about many things or argue or employ discursive thought he is made to concentrate with all his powers. This concentration reaches to saturation point, and then new energies hitherto undreamed of come into action, and, what is most important the true life is revealed of union with Buddha. The intellect, therefore, is in play, but not discursively. St. Thomas, on the other hand, takes the mind more pacifically and steadily from one range of thought to another. There are six steps, he says, "whereby we ascend by means of creatures to the contemplation of God. For the first step consists in the mere consideration of sensible objects; the second consists in going forward from sensible to intelligible objects; the third step is to judge of sensible objects according to intelligible things; the fourth is the absolute consideration of the intelligible objects to which one has attained by means of sense-data; the fifth is the contemplation of those intelligible objects that are unattainable by way of sense data, but which the reason is able to grasp; the sixth step is the consideration of such intelligible things as the reason can neither discover nor grasp, which pertain to the sublime contemplation of divine truth, wherein contemplation is ultimately perfected." Not that here St. Thomas is demanding each of these steps as a preliminary to contemplation. He is not, like the Buddhist, giving a technique, but rather showing the ordered process which a rational inquirer should follow. What the Buddhist teacher is doing resembles more the advice of a Thomas a Kempis or a St. John of the Cross to a novice in prayer. At the same time we must not press this difference too far. In all the great systems of Indian philosophy dependent on the Vedanta, whether of Sankara or Ramanuja or Madhva, the cultivation of knowledge is required. The mind has to meditate on its separation from matter and its relation to the divine being, and in time, too, it has to pass to a loving contemplation of its heavenly destiny. Plato, too, intended to lead his followers from the sensible and through a dialectic until the soul could behold the Form of the Good.

Contemplation, then, is at least different from "synthetic intuition" in emphasizing love. At the same time it seems to cut down gradually the part of intellect. It has no bias against intellect, but it seems gradually to be dispensing with it and drawing toward mysticism—the illuminative passing into the unitive way. The famous description given by St. Augustine in his *Confessions* brings together all the ingredients of contemplation just given above and is on the threshold or beyond it of mysticism. The steps he gives are not unlike those given, though more dryly, by St. Thomas—and it is safe to say that they are a Neo-Platonic heirloom. He tells first in Book Seven how he passed in meditation by stages from bodies to the soul, from the soul to its inner power, from that to reasoning about the mutable, and from thence he withdrew his mind "from its habitual way, abstracting from the confused crowds of phantasms that it might find what light suffused it, when with utter certainty it cried aloud that the immutable was to be preferred to the mutable, and how it had come to know the immutable itself. . . . Thus in the thrust of a trembling glance my mind arrived at That Which Is." But, as he says, he lacked the strength to hold his gaze fixed, and returned to his old habits. This first flight upward was only a rehearsal, and couched in Platonic language. The ripe moment came when he was with his mother, Monica, for the last time, "leaning in a window, which looked inwards to the garden within the house where we were staying at Ostia." They were talking "of the presence of Truth, which You are, and of eternal life." "And our conversation had brought us to this point that any pleasure whatsoever of the bodily senses, in any brightness whatsoever of corporeal light, seemed to us not worthy of comparison with the pleasures of that eternal Light, not worthy even of mention. Rising as our love flamed upward towards that Self-same, we passed in review the various levels of bodily things, up to the heavens themselves, whence sun and moon and stars shine upon this earth. And higher still we soared, thinking in our minds and speaking and marvelling at Your works; and so we came to our own souls, and went beyond them to come at last to that region of richness unending, where You feed Israel forever with the food of truth; and there life is that Wisdom by which all things are made, both the things that have been and the things that are yet to be. But this Wisdom itself is not made: it is as it ever has been, and so it shall be forever: indeed 'has ever been' and 'shall be forever' have no place in it, but it simply is, for it is eternal: whereas 'to have been' and 'to be going to be' are not eternal. And while we were thus talking of His Wisdom and panting for it, with all the effort of our heart we did for one instant attain to touch it: then sighing, and leaving the first fruits of our spirit bound to it, we returned to the sound of our own tongue, in which a word has both beginning and ending."

In this passage Wisdom is clearly an attribute of God, an aspect of Him who reveals himself gradually through shadows and images, and draws St. Augustine finally to the vision of the living Wisdom itself. In the first part St. Augustine describes the ascent of the mind from the mutable to the immutable, from the "brightness of corporeal light" to the eternal light. This procedure was in his time, and still is, a prescribed method of meditation and contemplation, and had nothing exceptional about it. But at the close of this part he has clearly the intention of telling us of something new, of a new and blissful experience, that is, to which before he has never fully attained. It is a kind of rapture, set however in intellectual terms. The mind is active but caught and stilled in the vision of Wisdom. So close and intimate is what he sees that "with a stirring of the heart" he is enabled to touch it. He seems to be saying that sight and touch, mind and heart, come together when the wisdom which he enjoys is his God. But the description is not without its difficulties. Dom Cuthbert Butler had to ask himself whether this is Platonic or Christian mysticism. The Neo-Platonists regarded ecstasy as the culminating experience of an *intellectual* process, and, so we are told, Porphyry once and Plotinus four times reached this state of ecstasy. Now that St. Augustine, whatever language he uses, had a different outlook from the Neo-Platonists is certain. The beginning and end of all to Plotinus was the One, and in the sixth Ennead he writes of the "flight of the alone to the Alone." St. Augustine knew this doctrine and repudiated it in favor of the worship and love of a living God.* In the very passage quoted above we can feel the quiver of emotion in the presence of a living Love. It looks as if, well read as he was in Neo-Platonic philosophy, he naturally and perforce took over its terminology to describe a different experience of his own. This shows how dangerous it is to identify experiences couched in similar language. In succeeding centuries many of the Christian mystics adopted the language of Denys the Areopagite, because they thought that he was a disciple of St. Paul; and as a result the account of their experiences has at times a Neo-Platonic flavor. What remains problematic is the part played by the intellect in their experiences, and, in particular, in that of St. Augustine. Wisdom of one kind or another can be reached in a synthetic or contemplative vision, in an intuition, or, if we take words literally, in an experience said to be utterly beyond thought. In each case love enters in, either as a partner or possibly as a sole agent. Mind and heart co-operate, with the mind dropping behind the closer the union attained. That is why many are disposed to place St. Augustine among the contemplatives instead of among

* The Christian mystics attribute all that they receive to the supernatural gift of divine grace.

the mystics proper. The mystics do use the language of sight, and in the Christian tradition keep the intellect in commission. Heaven consists, in Scriptural terms, of seeing "God face to face," as He is; but they prefer the language of touch. They are passive and "suffer" the presence and action of another upon them, and are slain by love. In reaching toward this experience the mystic does not, like St. Augustine, consider creatures as stepping stones; he turns his back upon them. He forsakes the half lights to find the uncreated light, and enters into the cloud of unknowing. The reward is that overwhelming experience, which can be likened to nothing which he has known before. So at variance, indeed, is it with all the assertions of common sense and with the judgments of the so-called wise that he is tempted to dismiss these as foolish and make of his experience the test of all truth and the one value which is worth pursuing.

This is the wisdom which Coomaraswamy and Aldous Huxley pronounce to be the one unitive force in East and West. Those who live in busy cities may dismiss it as too esoteric or as demanding too much of human nature. They forget that in one form or another it has appealed to countless millions in the East. Here now, too, in the West there are conditions which favor its rebirth. The old, comfortable, bourgeois satisfaction with life and "the way things were going," is over. We are back in an age of uncertainty and ingratitude, and are in fear of not "counting" or of being unrecognized. Dr. J. Lopez Ibor in *Faith, Reason and Modern Psychiatry* tells us that "when we interrogate an anxious person in detail, we always stumble upon two types of fear: fear of going mad and fear of death." Our personality and our existence are threatened by the menace of death and a disregarding universe or fate. In the words of W. H. Auden:

> The ambiguity of progress,
> The enlightenment driven away,
> The habit-forming pain,
> Mismanagement and grief:
> We must suffer them all again.

A credible answer to this problem lies at hand. If then there are to be found in the history of all the important religious philosophies of the world groups of teachers who practice what they preach, and have inspired large groups to imitate their own way of life; and if again in all these philosophies there is a remarkable family likeness; then they deserve the attention of all as possibly having the key to truth about the nature of human existence. Now, as Mr. Aldous Huxley argues, it is agreed by many that these religious philosophers are indeed at one in their answer to the questions which most torment men, answers, which have been tested by long meditation and discipline of mind, and bearing upon the meaning of the material world, the human self, its purposes and destiny and the nature of ultimate reality. They were thought wise in their generation, and they have left in writing an expression of their experience and thought. It is not unreasonable, therefore, to call their testimony to the perfect life the perennial wisdom, marking out, as it does, the errors to which man is prone and the true path of salvation to be followed.

The thoughts which most torment man arise out of what is now called his "existentialist predicament." The sensitive, conscious being, which is man, is confronted by a world, inscrutable and indifferent, one in which he cannot call his soul his own. The material world reduces him to its own level; he is part of its drive and its dust, and he moves inevitably according to its rhythms, fastened to a wheel of fate. This wheel is the recurring image, in ancient literatures, of man's lot. The religious sages accepted this symbol of human bondage, but taught the means of deliverance. The popular stories and the myths refer to demons, archontes and cosmocrators, who ultimately are conquered by the beneficent powers. Here is the harlequinade, which expresses, far more than the authors and players themselves know, the pathos of man in that he feels caught and seeks release. Behind the myth is the realization that the soul in its essence is above matter and time and all the laws of fate. Dr. Mircea Eliade says of these myths of time and its cycles that they reveal to us "the ontological irreality of the universe and the path of our deliverance." The Gnostic, the Buddhist and the Hindu, even the Neo-Platonist, have one and the same theme, that deliverance lies in the contemplative and intuitive life and in the ascetical and mystical techniques which introduce us to it. The Hindu does, however, grant an indulgence and salvage the active life. The active life can serve as a path to wisdom, provided that its fruits and joys are at each moment renounced. We may act as if this life counted, as long as we recognize at the same time that it has no value or substance. "Time can become an instrument of knowledge in the sense that it serves to project a thing or a being onto the plane of cosmic time, and thereby convince us of its irreality." This is the sop for the majority of men, who otherwise would dwell in exterior darkness; and the lines which they can follow are laid down in a work such as the Bhagavad-Gita. This concession does not however conflict with the central doctrine of deliverance.

In his introduction to the Mentor edition of the Bhagavad-Gita Aldous Huxley gives a clear résumé of this common wisdom; the highest common factor, as he calls it, of the great religious writings. Despite the varying traditions and sundering influences and the topical additions which differentiate these writings, he believes that in them there is present a perennial philosophy in its "chemically pure state." These writings include the Vedanta and Hebrew prophecy, the Tao Teh Ching and the Platonic dialogues, the Gospel according to St. John and Mahayana theology, Plotinus and the Areopagite, the Persian Sufis and the Christian mystics of the Middle Ages and the Renaissance. He sums up what is common to all these writings under four heads. First: all the phenomena of nature and of our individualized consciousness are the manifestation of a Divine Ground. Second: human beings can know this Divine Ground not only by inference but by a direct intuition, and in so intuiting it they enter into unity with it. Third: human beings have a double nature, a phenomenal ego and a spirit which is really a spark of divinity. Because of this latter they can identify themselves with the Divine Ground. Fourth: the one aim of life on earth must be to find this unity in and identification with the Divine Ground by means of intuitive knowledge. In Hinduism Brahman is this Divine Ground, and in Mahayana Buddhism it is called Mind or the Pure Light or the Void. Amongst Christian teachers who hold this view, Eckhart, Ruysbroeck and Suso are cited. The second doctrine is even more universally manifest. All the great religions teach that there is a higher form of knowledge than discursive reasoning, and it consists of an experience which brings the spirit into unity with God or the Divine Ground. With the third doctrine of the dual nature of man Aldous Huxley has a more difficult passage. All the higher religions, he asserts, admit it. They all teach the need of self-abnegation and charity. So far, so good. This implies, he then goes on to say, that only by these means "can we clear away the evil, folly and ignorance which constitute the thing we call our personality and prevent us from becoming aware of the spark of divinity illuminating the inner man." But as Christianity denies this identification, and "the Sufi, Mansur, was executed for giving to the words 'union and identification' the literal meaning which they bear in the Hindu tradition," he calls their theology a rationalization of the empirical fact, namely, the intuitive experience of union. As to the final end of man, the identification of the self with its "eternal self" and the intuitive knowledge of the divine Ground, we are told that "all the higher religions are in complete agreement."

Here then we have the highest common factor, the "chemically pure state," which constitutes the perennial wisdom. It is a wisdom which must be sought with the whole heart and mind, and a long novitiate is required before it can be attained. In this pursuit the moral virtues provide the essential prerequisites; for action and knowledge help each other out, and the self must strip itself of all its illusions, its possessiveness and selfishness. That is why non-attachment or "holy indifference," as some of the Christian writers call it, and love are taught by all the sages of East and West. Aldous Huxley contrasts the busy, practical outlook of modern Western civilization with this other world philosophy. He notes the absence of quiet and contemplation in the syllabus of education and culture, the preference for what is practical and for immediate results, and he concludes that nothing is more necessary for even temporal peace and happiness than the restoration of the balance and the return of the high regard for religious contemplation and the quiet of mind which heralds the coming of the kingdom of the spirit. That mankind should ignore the evidence which Aldous Huxley and others have put together, and even disdain the experiences accumulated from all quarters of the world and from all times, which are far too general and too similar to be dismissed as an accident, is as mysterious as the folly of those who run after tyrants and clap at the news of their own imbecility and coming perdition. I have heard it said by a distinguished modern philosopher that the only evidence for the spirit of man as against his purely animal constitution lies in the new evidence of paranormal phenomena. Telepathy and second sight can bring deliverance from the wheel of necessity and predetermined behaviorism, whereas the Bhagavad-Gita and Ruysbroeck are overheated in imagination and belong to the category of the manic or abnormal! The philosophers of our day have no care for such evidence of what man is and might be. As Professor Brand Blanshard says in his lecture to the British Academy: "The new philosophy is more intimately connected than the old with mathematics and natural science, and less intimately with literature, art, and religion; it sets comparatively little store by the history of philosophy, which, consisting largely of metaphysics, is chiefly a chronicle of confusion; and since it regards the search for a *summum bonum* as also confusion, ethic has turned its attention from the end of life either to reviewing the forms of behavior or to analyzing the language of our emotions about them. Among the qualities required of the philosopher, those that used to be summed up under culture play a smaller role, while logical subtlety and acuteness play a larger role. This means in turn that philosophy is losing some part of that connotation of *wisdom* that it once carried."

Whatever then be said about the inner consistency of the perennial philosophy proposed by Aldous Huxley, Guénon and others, as an essay, and a constant essay of the human spirit to satisfy the mind and the heart, it defies the limitations imposed on man by any materialistic or purely humanistic ideals. Time and space, however much they contribute to joy and virtue and social happiness, are felt, as experience proves, to be like a film over the eyes and a fetter to the feet. The one is described as a wheel or cycle to which man is bound, the other as a barrier which frustrates the unity sought in knowledge and love. When Plato disparaged sensible reality, saying that it was half unreal, that it was never the same, coming and disappearing, the shadowy appearance of something we could not grasp, he had to meet the incredulity of those who feel that the one thing certain is the hard ground under their feet, the palpable, visible world we can sense. Now, however, science has moved to a position of wonder and doubt about the steadfastness of the physical universe. This world keeps changing its face and makes all our calculations about it relative. The moving hand writing on the wall can never be interpreted, and so convinced of this are many modern philosophers that they cling to a happy-go-lucky "common sense" and admit that neither the laws nor concepts of science need have any direct counterpart in the actual world. Among the philosophers an analysis of language has taken the place of an investigation into the nature of things; the differential calculus is the new alchemy. As the scientist, however, keeps near to nature in practice, there is always hope that he may, like St. Augustine, find it a pedagogue to wisdom; but neither the existentialist, who throws up the sponge, nor the analysts of language have much to offer which compares with the highest common factor of knowledge and experience laid before us by the perennial philosophers.

The great danger of the latter is that they arrange together jewels which may at first sight look alike, but are on inspection very different. I began this chapter with the problem of the connection of contemplative knowledge and mystical experience. It will be observed that Aldous Huxley, in the interests perhaps of brevity, does not distinguish between them. There are other obscurities in his account. He chooses as the most convenient description of the full and ultimate reality what he calls the "Divine Ground." He says that it is creative, sustaining and transforming, and it is not clear how such a Ground can fulfill all these activities. The Christian mystics do at times use some such description, but hardly in the same final sense in which it is used in Hinduism; and in the Moslem tradition such a description is suspect. There is a similar ambiguity over the manner in which the highest experience is gained. It is called "intuition," a higher form of knowledge and identification. An intuition does seem by its very nature to call for a subject or agent who sees or has a direct vision, so that however close the unity of the object and subject becomes there remain two. But where there is identification there is only one remaining. In the third doctrine of this perennial philosophy we are told that the double nature of man is affirmed in "all the higher religions." Huxley goes on from this to declare that, by denying our lower self and concentrating on the higher, we realize that this higher is a spark of divinity. We thus get rid of this personality of ours and come to the intuitive knowledge of our real life, which is one with the Divine Ground. Now this doctrine as so explained is not easy to follow, and as a philosophy it raises great problems. How is it that what is really divine can so forget itself as to believe in its finiteness and in its unity with a lower reality, and how can this apparent unity, which makes up our personality, have any rational meaning at all? What again is this lower self and what is this nature around us, which appears to have its own reality, but is in fact some kind of illusion? In a philosophy such as that of Hegel's, some attempt is made to explain why there are, as it seems, different levels of reality, and why nature and all that lies on the object side of thought appear to be estranged from us. But such attempts can hardly be judged to be successful, and for this reason among others, that neither the existence of evil nor of finite nature qua finite is adequately explained. In this kind of view all that we normally think real gradually fades out, and we are in the end what we must always have been, namely, a spark of divinity. At the present time a new interest has developed in history, and there is a great desire to give it a meaning and purpose. In the great religions of the East time is of no account and history is a phantom. In the Christian religion, on the other hand, history has an essential role and Christianity cannot be understood without it. In keeping with this respect for history Christianity is concerned with the growth of man and of the part which each single man plays in it. Huxley tells us that all the great religions advocate self-denial and charity, and it is certainly true that in them the silver must be cleaned of its tarnish, the light freed from its smoky shade. But this is not enough. Personality must be stripped from us so that we emerge in our true godhead. Self-denial, therefore, is to be understood literally, and not in the Christian sense of subduing our lower nature to the purposes of the higher and then subduing our will to the will of God. *Cui servire regnare est.* In other words, there is this difference between the Christian and the Hindu or Buddhist conception of self-denial, that the former aims to keep the person, the latter to dissolve it.

Like self-denial, charity also can be understood in different senses. So impressed have many Western thinkers been by the teaching of Buddhism on "maitri," which they translate as "charity," that they identify it with Christian charity. Thus Renouvier wrote: "That the sovereign precept of Buddhism is a law of absolute love, perfect charity . . . exactly like the precept of the gospels." Much that is written about it certainly has a beauty fit to steal the heart away; on the other hand, it must be confessed that some of the stories told are childish and absurd. But it would be a grave mistake to confuse the Buddhist teaching with the Christian. The maitri of the Buddhist is only a preliminary to a state which is beyond it, a point of departure and not the end of life, a means, therefore, and not an end. In this world of illusion the Buddhist novice must begin with an infinite pity for all that belongs to it, the suffering and the evil, but as he comes to contemplation, to greater and greater indifference and finally to complete serenity, he frees himself from all these illusions. "When Yasa was seated beside him, the Blessed one taught him by degrees: that is to say; he told him first about charity (dana), of morality (sila) and of the heavenly rewards (svarga); and then of the misery and vanity and the blemish of desires, and of the happiness which the renunciation of desires brings." And again: "Just as the stem of the banana tree, when decomposed into its parts, does not exist, so the 'I,' looked at critically, is found to be pure nothingness.—If the individual does not exist, on what then will compassion exercise itself? It is imagined to be by an illusion which one adopts in view of the end which is to be attained." This end is that serenity which is attained in absorption into the Buddha. As a consequence charity is a mode of purification of the self, and with the gradual purging of all desires charity too is dissolved in the void where all is peace. Even during the formation of the Buddhist adept, during the period of the stripping of illusion, what is called charity is rather a pity and compassion than what the Christian means by love, and there are degrees in this compassion. The lowest and most vulgar is that felt for those who suffer, and it is the lowest because there the illusion is the greatest. It supposes the reality of suffering persons. The next degree is that felt for the distress and the suffering. This is higher because no longer is there the belief in the reality of personal life. But this still is coated with error and must be succeeded by perfect compassion which has no object. It is an ideal pity, free from the affection for persons, free too from all desire to alleviate suffering, and at its highest it has no subject or object; it is, so to speak, the pure condition of compassion. Such a condition is far removed from what Christianity understands by charity. "Little children love one another." Love is not just a taking off from the ground or a scaffolding to be discarded. It is the end and consummation of the religious ideal, and it is between persons. Faith and hope will pass away, says St. Paul, but not charity. God himself is love, St. John tells us, and the two commandments are that we shall love God and love our neighbor. The fundamental difference between this and the Buddhist conception lies in the respective attitude to persons. To the Christian God is personal, and creates out of love and raises his creatures to a union of love with Himself; and between creatures love is mutual; it is an exchange in which each loves the other for himself and gives himself to the other. There is no illusion here; it is not part of a purgation of self nor a passing, if necessary, phase in the self's pursuit of the Whole, the dipping into the Divine Ground.

The traits, therefore, in the higher religions cited by Aldous Huxley which at a first glance look alike reveal on closer inspection profound differences. It would be possible to divide them into two classes, those which are all pointed to a personal God, such as Christianity, Judaism and Islam, and those which make nought of all which they think to lack absolute perfection. Hinduism and Buddhism and the main series of Gnostic beliefs are so conscious of the imperfection of human living and so stirred to rise above it that they treat what is natural and human as an unsubstantial image, as an illusion from which they can be delivered. There is undeniable beauty in the path of deliverance as set forth by the sages of the East, and so convincing is the ideal contained in their message that many of the practical and empirical philosophies of today are made to look like bourgeois folly. That certain aspects, too, of all these religions should look so akin and actually concur with one another at certain points almost warrants us in calling their wisdom one without more ado and treating it as a lasting record of the highest experiences of mankind. The end may be different, but in the desire for deliverance from the treadmill of the human prison, with its sorrows and unrewarding pleasures, and the plague of egotism and loneliness, all the wise are united.

> Restless man's mind is,
> So strongly shaken
> In the grip of the senses:
> Gross and grown hard
> With stubborn desire
> For what is worldly.
> How shall he tame it?
> Truly, I think,
> The wind is no wilder.*

But:

> The devoted dwell with Him,
> They know Him always
> There in the heart,
> Where action is not.
> He is all their aim.
> Made free by His knowledge
> From past uncleanness
> Of deed or of thought,
> They find the place of freedom,
> The place of no return.†

Such poetry belongs to the greatest religious tradition, and the language used is a common heritage. Indeed the language

---

* From the *Bhagavad-Gita,* translated by Christopher Isherwood and Swami Prabhavananda, copyright 1951 by The Vedanta Society of Southern California.

† *Ibid.*

used, as for instance in the Bhagavad-Gita, is applicable to the teaching of all the wise, and so tends to hide variance of view. What is more personal than such a stanza as the following:

> Give me your whole heart,
> Love and adore me,
> Worship me always,
> Bow to me only,
> And you shall find me:
> This is my promise
> Who love you dearly.
> Lay down all duties
> In me, your refuge.
> Fear no longer,
> For I will save you
> From sin and from bondage.*

Similarly, amongst the Christian mystics we find a language at times so impersonal that it cannot be distinguished from that of the Hindu or Buddhist philosopher. This is a point on which Guénon and Huxley have seized, and as it is a crucial one I must dwell on it at greater length.

* *Ibid.*

III.

Eastern and Western Mysticism

THE Greek Fathers of the Church naturally turned to the Hellenic philosophers for assistance in clarifying and articulating the theology contained in the Christian Revelation. In the West St. Augustine was foremost in translating pagan ideas into Christian terms; he set an example which led in time to the systematizations of the medieval school. That is why his account of his spiritual experience given above has a special importance in a survey of Christian and pagan wisdom. In that account ordinary thought passes into vision or intuition, and vision is warmed by love. A similar language is used by all the mystics, except that many of them go further, throw away knowledge altogether and speak of a complete identity of being with the object loved and worshiped. This partial similarity of language is illuminating; it can also be deceptive. All the mystics tell us that their experience is ineffable, and this is obvious in the sense, at least, that none of the words which fit our common experience can do it justice. They are bound, therefore, in their attempt to communicate with us, to fall back on a limited variety of metaphors and analogies. It must be remembered that their descriptions are written when the experience is over, and that the words a mystic uses will be those familiar to him from tradition and from the writings he knows. For the thought which is so far above his normal thinking he falls back upon "vision" or "intuition"; and for love's delights he has recourse to "fusion" or "absorption." "I *saw* eternity the other night . . ."; "To *see* the world in a grain of sand . . ."; "In the serene night with the flame that consumes, and gives no pains." Poetic vision is, indeed, a semblance of the mystic.

Emerson in a passage on "The Poet" tells us how, while we are accustomed to dealing with symbols and the economic use of things, the poet advances to an intellectual perception. "As the eyes of Lyncaeus were said to see through the earth, so the poet turns the world to glass, and shows us all things in their right series and procession." Emerson here exaggerates the gift of the poet because it is the imagination taking off from the sensible which is at work, whereas intuition proper is the intellect streamlined and at full power. It comes when the mind catches sight of truth as directly as the eye sees color. The sages and the mystics after long self-denial and concentration, when the multiplicity of images has been discarded and the spiritual eye is clear and suitably focused, are privileged to see what Plato calls Beauty itself, the Buddhists the Pure Land, or Denys the splendor of inaccessible light.

The characteristics of this intuition, then, are that it is direct and immediate, and that it beholds the object seen as it really is. It can also be described as a possession of the object, for the object is no longer at a distance, no longer severed by any obstacle from the knower. Indeed the philosophers go on to say that this is the highest form of union conceivable. The mind to them is the unique instrument of truth, and therefore of union, the most delicate as well as the most intimate way of entering into relation with what is not the self. This may be a natural prejudice of the professional thinkers, the adepts of mind, whereas the advocates of love have another story to tell. The philosophers can make out a strong case. What they say is: that what I know is truly mind and a part of myself, and when all the doors of separation to be found in ordinary human intercourse have been broken down, then there is nothing between the subject and the object; the object lives in the very knowing of the subject and is part of his life. Such a unity is the highest possible, and there are no longer any secrets hidden from the sight. It should be noted that the natural image for describing such an intuition is that of sight. It is in the spiritual and intellectual order what sight is in the sensible, and for the same reason the first word which comes to the mind to describe the object is beauty. Perfect being is seen in all its superessential splendor. On the other hand when we turn to the mystical experience the natural language seems to be not so much of sight as of contact, presence and the "wending into one." The sense of presence is an important feature, and at the same time difficult to analyze, and its importance has been too often neglected. We talk loosely of things as present to us, though more naturally as being present before our eyes, but the usage of the term is better confined to living beings and most appropriately to persons. We can sense the presence of a person in the room, and we are affected by it. In religious writings awe and fright are caused by the impression of a divine presence. *Apparent dirae facies;* the presence of the god in the wood causes panic. "How fearsome is this place; surely this is no other than the house of God." Instead, then, of being free in our loneliness to say and do what we like, we experience in the presence of another the pressure of his contact and are in varying degrees made passive by it. Now in the mystic experience we are made aware of the presence of another. God being a spirit and beyond ordinary experience, we normally converse with him indirectly. Out of our knowledge and faith come the prayers which we address to him; in such ordinary experience we experience his absence and know his presence. But at a moment in the contemplative life this condition begins to change, and whereas before we had to be active, concentrating our mind and keeping ourselves attentive to what we know is true, now something akin to what happens when another person comes into the room and speaks to us begins. We have to listen and be passive, to experience presence, the loving presence of one who is all in all to us. This is what is meant by experimental union, the description usually given of mystical experience.

If intuition be of sight and mystical experience of presence, it can be held that the former is of things, of concrete universals and of the impersonal or transpersonal, whereas the latter is related to persons and their meeting. The one is more suited to the "I"-thing relation, and the other to the "I"-"Thou" relation. In the one we see and possess, in the other we belong to the lover, who plays upon us as a musician plays upon an instrument. But this is too simple an account, for love and intellect belong to both experiences, though the accent in each is different. M. Maritain in his *Creative Intuition in Art and Poetry* stresses the fact that even in poetic experience love and knowledge go together. He quotes De Quincey: "The Scriptures themselves never condescended to deal by suggestion or co-operation with the mere discursive understanding; when speaking of man in his intellectual capacity, the Scriptures speak not of the understanding, but of *'the understanding heart'*—making the heart, i.e. the great *intuitive* (or non discursive) organ, to be the interchangeable formula for man in his highest state of capacity for the infinite." It is either an understanding heart or an affectionate understanding. Love gives insight and the intuition of the wise is no cold penetration into the nature of the object but a complete sympathy of understanding. In all experience an external object sets up a reaction of the self, sometimes so weak or mild as to leave it indifferent. If interest be aroused there is the desire to use or benefit by the object and the experience, or again on a higher level curiosity or admiration awakens. In the presence of beauty a special joy arises, and akin to this is the desire of the artist to seek himself in terms of the object, and so he creates what is his own, though emotionally what he sees fuses with his own creation. The bell has been rung by an outsider and with that ring other sounds have been touched off. The artist through his sensibility and affection divines more in the object than others see, and dances his own dance before it. Even here, however, he behaves differently according as knowledge or love predominates. March Phillipps has pointed out in his *Form and Colour* how there are two moods to be found throughout the development of art, "the emotional mood, the mood of passive receptivity, in which insight is an integral part of feeling," and it is "not only different from the rational and intellectual mood, but is dispelled by rational and intellectual definitions in just the same way as the emotional effects of colour are dispelled by the intrusion of rigidly defined forms." Form in art is imposed on a recalcitrant material; it is intellectual and Apolline, whereas color and light and shade as seen for instance in much Byzantine work are emotional and Dionysiac; they win the heart of the beholder and take him out of himself. The reaction of the intellect to the object is to make it its own, to grasp and possess it, and its end is achieved when the object has taken form in the mind and enriched the mind. On the other hand the object may allure the self. When it rings the bell, then "all the bells in Arundel ring"; the self is entranced and slips away from the house in the dark to meet the lover.

These two moods of which March Phillipps writes are particular forms which the two original sources of energy in the self take. They and other human experiences are like tributaries which can be traced back to two ultimate loves. One is centripetal, the other centrifugal, making the self face within and without, like the god Janus. As with all other living things the human self grows to be itself more and more, and so by its very nature it seeks its own well-being; this is the root of life. But the self is not complete by itself; it is part of a species and of the universe, and, let us say, it comes forth from God and returns to him. Hence there is a movement away from its own self-interest, an identification of itself with what is beyond, a herd instinct, a mass emotion, a self-surrender, what Freud has diagnosed as a death instinct. In the animal world we see these two impulses at work in the struggle for existence, the brute force of the male and the passivity of the female. In human life there is the cruel, almost animal craving for power, the dominance of one over multitudes, and the mysterious gratification of so many in abandoning themselves to the will of another and in losing themselves in a Dionysiac religious frenzy. Fully humanized the possessive impulse shows itself in self-respect, independence, growth of personality and especially in the pursuit of knowledge, where the godlike reason introduces form, order, and organization into its world without and within. The self-giving impulse on its part shows itself in communal acts, fellow-feeling, labor without reward and self-sacrificing love. As the possessive love is seen in its noonday beauty in Greek art and philosophy it has been called, not altogether wisely, Eros, and the name Agape, taken from the New Testament, has been given to the other in its highest manifestations.

Eros is most conspicuous in the activity of knowing, and consequently in intuition, but it is subdued and mellowed in religious intuition by the presence of Agape. The mind is reinforced by a current of sympathy set up between the object and the subject; the latter listens while searching or holding and enters into collusion with the object. This kind of "connaturality" is seen on lower levels in the responses of critics to works of art or philosophical writings. One onlooker is quick to see what the artist or author intends, the while a supposedly much more intellectually gifted critic cannot make head or tail of what is before him. The self-giving lover, on the other hand, is all the while outside himself. His ego does not get in the way, and here lies his peril. The wild excesses of love, manias of self-abandonment, of self-mutilation, the monstrous mass hysterias, which have been all too frequent in history, bear witness to this danger. This love reaches to the heights in ecstasy and self-giving; it also descends into dark places. So much attention has been given in recent years to the workings of the unconscious, and so much evidence has been collected and sifted of witchcraft, magical rites and religious prayer techniques that we can begin at any rate to map out the underground of natural religion and mysticism. Ethnologists tell us that primitive man lived almost somnambulistically and co-consciously with his tribe the rhythm of day and night and of the seasons, and this rhythm corresponded with the two impulses of assertiveness and gaining self and of losing it. The psychologists, also, have pointed out the all-pervading symbolism of water and earth. The self descends into the one and is covered by the other. As in the Christian service of Tenebrae the candles are removed one by one from the triangular candlestick until the church is left in darkness, so the self is drawn into the dark, and no final light may be brought from behind the altar as a sign of resurrection. The familiar marks of the self are obliterated, Absalom hangs by his hair from a tree and the maiden becomes a perquisite of the temple. In everyday life we can watch the impulse at work, when "the individual personality really risks being dissolved into the unconscious of the mass; the individual gradually loses his distinctive features, his personal thoughts, his own character." But in natural mysticism the self is drawn to its ultimate destiny by a profound self-abnegation, and here the symbols of water and earth have their special place. P. Louis Beirnaert in *The Mythic Dimension in Christian Sacramentalism* quotes evidence far and wide of the mystic symbolism of water. "It is death for souls to become water" (Heraclitus), or as an Indian text states: "Water, you are the source of everything and of all existence." The self returns to its source, and immersed in water loses its identity, as in a maternal womb. The early Fathers of the Church recognized this symbolism in the waters of baptism, and saw in the grace conferred the victory over the powers of this earth and the waters. The earth, too, is a mother, and poets as well as natural mystics have spontaneously thought of it as such.

Rationalists, who, following the Cartesian tradition, make a sharp cut between the mind and the body and put their entire trust in the reasonable self, have to turn a blind eye to the phenomena of the unconscious. A longer-enduring philosophy, which indeed is nearer to deserving the name "perennial," can and does integrate the unconscious into its system. In this system the spirit and the body make one human being, and so intimate is the interrelation between the two that the influence of both can be discerned in what looks to be either the most spiritual or the most sensible of human experiences. The mind is by its nature immaterial, and theoretically its sole object is the truth about the real world and itself. In practice, however, as the whole self is the subject, it is seldom, if ever, entirely free from feeling, desire, emotion and interest, from the temporal and spatial setting, which comes from the senses and imagination and memory and gives individuality to what is being considered by the mind. Moreover, what is immediate in experience passes out of conscious awareness, but clearly remains in some form which can be revived again in memory. What we are contains far more than is given to us at any particular moment in full awareness, and this garnered experience is still active in methods of reaction, in habits and moods and in devious ways which have been more and more brought to light by recent psychological investigation. As contrasted with conscious awareness this mass of experience in reserve and night-watching has been given the name of the subconscious and the unconscious (a not too happy description because what is brought to light has to be described in terms almost identical with those of conscious awareness, except that this conscious awareness is absent). This may be inevitable, but it is unfortunate as it accustoms us to thinking of the unconscious as if it were conscious, a mindless subterranean world with all the trappings of mind. It might be better to employ the distinction of consciousness and self-consciousness. Self-consciousness is our habitual waking state; we are aware of what we are doing, saying and thinking; there is a constant interior dialogue between the I observing and the I acting, the one disengaged, the other busy about many things, and this dialogue may be of a high or low intensity. The one self is hardly in communication with the other in states of reverie, and in dreams the relation is disturbed, the disengaged I being, as it were, tied and at the mercy of the otherself. In deep sleep and in times of amnesia or so-called unconsciousness, we suppose that we have really lost consciousness, and we say that our minds and wills are there—because we are not dead—but only potentially active. But can a mind ever be inactive, and what can be the meaning of a potential thought other than an incomplete thought? Thinking either is or is not there at all. What then the modern psychologist means by the unconscious may be the mass of thoughts and desires to the recording of which I cannot pay attention. Communication is dependent on so many factors, psycho-physical as well as psychical. As among the very old memory can become so defective that the same question or remark will be repeated as soon as it is finished, so the I is unable to record and memorize the thoughts as they stream past it. The mind is always conscious, but self-consciousness may be vivid or dim or in a blackout. Now besides the experience which the individual has acquired in his life history and which is still active behind the stage, psychotherapy claims to bring to light experiences of which the individual could never have been conscious. These are said to belong to the "collective unconscious." Such a description begs many questions, and at best can only be called a working hypothesis, one which brings together under a heading some of the mysterious phenomena of human life and the mysterious patterns which myths invariably follow. Jung thinks of this "collective unconscious" as the precipitate of the experience of all mankind. As the body has in it vestiges of its various stages of development, so there are correspondences among all human beings from all quarters of the world and from all ages which give a mental structure analogous to that of the bodily structure. Another way of describing this unconscious is to liken it to patterns of behavior, "functional engrams in which the age-old experience of mankind is crystallized and which lead people into typical patterns of behaviour. They do not consist of inherited ideas but of inherited predispositions to reaction."

We are told by the ethnologists that primitive man lived a tribal life more than an individual one, that his consciousness was still for the most part tied to the nature in the midst of which he lived and to the communal life of the tribe. In this primitive life Malinowski tells us that the myth was not a mere tale told but a reality lived. The myth was "the assertion of an original, greater, and more important reality through which the present life, fate, and work of mankind" were governed. The psychologist develops this idea of the ethnologist further and maintains that the myth is also the projection of the life which the primitive is living, the unconscious taking form in soul-stirring images. He feels pulsating through him the source of life, the unity which makes him both one with nature and separate from it. Dr. Kerenyi suggests that his origin is expressed in the mythology of the child and of the woman goddess. As the individual is always aware of his precarious hold upon his separate selfhood he tends to regress in times of danger, and in obedience to the centrifugal impulse seeks to lose himself in the embrace of the dark goddess. This is one of the sources of natural mysticism, of the cult of the Magna Mater and of that worship of the earth which is to be seen in Richard Jefferies and at times in D. H. Lawrence. Kerenyi calls it the grounding of the self, where the self loses itself and at the same time finds its own center in "the abyss of the nucleus." He is writing of the interior source of myth and not of natural mysticism, but what is true of the one is true of the other. This center or "abyss" is symbolized in the Roman custom, to which reference has already been made, of creating, at the foundation of a city, in the center a *mundus* or round pit consecrated to the Di Manes, the spirits of ancestors and of the underworld; it was made so as to appear like the vault of heaven to those looking down on it. What the pious but not mystical Romans had at the back of their minds in this symbolism is made clearer by a similar practice of the Buddhists. In their monasteries floors take the form of a circle with an open lotus leaf. "In it the contemplative sees himself standing in the form of Mahasukha (one of the great god Siva's manifestations), holding a female figure in his embrace. He sees himself as the highest bliss of the circles' . . . and becomes aware of his own essence through contemplation."

Mythology and the symbolic expressions of the unconscious,

when examined by analytical psychologists, give support, then, to the idea that in natural mysticism the self in total surrender has the sense of being united in a darkness to a vast reality, ineffable and divine, in which it loses its identity. The myths play round this idea, in the stories of Persephone and the Earth Goddess, and in the Eleusinian mysteries and the rites of Isis. But if this were all, the descent would be into the depths of the unconscious, and much of the beauty and sublimity of the mystic state described would be unintelligible. Kerenyi provides a positive element when he says that in the immersion of the self in its ground a movement to the spiritual is also discoverable, what he calls "a compulsion towards the spiritual." "The being of anything that grows is as much an exposure to something as an arising from something," and this something is spiritual. What this means, I suggest, is that no matter what the degree of self-annihilation or ecstasy, the self, with its other side, still hankers after knowledge and its own perfection, and therefore grows, or still more probably, God is drawing the soul to himself and making his presence felt:

> . . . Thou from the first
> Wast present, and, with mighty wings outspread,
> Dove-like satst brooding on the vast Abyss.

In an article in the *Hibbert Journal* Dr. R. L. Raehner remarks that "the Hindu attempt to combine an intense devotion to a personal God with a purely monist philosophy is certainly a *tour de force,* but it could be dangerous in that it tends to divide the personality into two." This conjunction of an impersonal absolute with hymns to and invocations of a personal God is indeed most striking. I have already quoted the exquisite poem from the Song of God, Bhagavad-Gita, beginning, "Give me your whole heart," and there are many more songs and prayers almost equally beautiful, and so sublime as to place their aspirations among the highest utterances of religion. Heart and mind are working together as they should do, and must do when in relation to the living God, and they contradict what the mind by itself, with its impersonal philosophizing, and the heart with its wild passion for sacrifice and funeral pyres, each in its turn proclaims. Man left to himself and brooding on his destiny can with his mind spin a texture of thought, which remains to the end an object and a piece of logic; it is lifeless and does not bleed. He can, again, in the Zen technique of concentration reach to a point when the self blends with the object; all his powers are gathered together in an active and passive awareness; he goes through a period of increasing tension until at the ripe moment his whole self and outlook are transformed. This is the moment "for you to cast aside the scabbard, throw yourself into the abyss, and by doing so lay a foundation for Buddhahood." This "wisdom" is the contribution which the East can bring to the West, which is busied about many things and inattentive to the call of the spirit. The path has its dangers; but even though the self, when left in the void, runs the risk of losing its identity, God can bring to the prepared mind a loftiness of soul and a purity of will which are a kind of pedagogue to his real presence—a Gulf Stream warming all those who sail upon its waters.

God is not a thing, nor a nameless absolute, nor a whole. Being alive he enters into a living relationship with persons, a relationship of "I-Thou" and not "I-It." The abstract and the impersonal, no matter how noble and infinite in connotation, are marks of human infirmity, and not signposts of perfection. That is why the two impulses of mastery and donation tend to fall apart or mix badly when the self is left to its own devices and lives in a void. The self is hypnotized by the void and plunges into it or gives it a positive significance which it does not possess. No wonder that Aldous Huxley found that he could enjoy an experience hardly distinguishable from a "mystical" state by administering a drug to himself. The dream or mystic world of the self has to be shaken by contact with a real person if its loves are to come together and sing "in harmony with truth." In the great silence induced by prayer and bodily techniques there are many forces, friendly and hostile, which gather round the soul. The "waters have lifted up their voice," the earth becomes the womb of being, and the words *beauty* and *goodness* are like soft music to the mind. This is the witching time of night, a foretaste, perhaps of happiness, but not the consummation. The word spoken in the night or the footstep of Another is far more precious, for it is living and loving. Only a living God can end the isolation of a person, and only another person can stretch out a saving hand to a self which is being carried away in the ocean of being. Man is not made to be alone. Deprived of companionship he loses the sense of his own worth and that of others, and comes to think of personality as an illusion and of the self as being a part of something greater, a passing illustration of the light that never was on sea or land. This is why the love of self and the self-denying love can be reconciled only—and that in part—in the mutual love of two persons, and finally in the love of God for man. As I have written in another place, we live in a community, and it is in that community that we "first discover others and salute them and address them as persons, as beings and persons who are most decidedly not ourselves, who demand of us that we treat them as beings who possess their own inalienable individuality and perfection. We are drawn to them not as being in any sense our own; it is just because they cannot be exploited or used or partitioned out that we attend to them for what they are in themselves. And here something happens. In loving things there is only a one-way street of love. We take and hold; the thing is ours or we lose ourselves in something bigger and disappear, and that is all. But in the relation of persons there is a return of love. Both are active and the mode of taking is to receive from another, and the more one gives the more one is likely to receive. I live by his life and he lives by mine." *

Both philosophy and experience bear out the truth that so far from personality being an illusion it is the highest of all categories. In the relation of the whole to its parts there is a noticeable change in accord with the ascending order of nature. In the inanimate world the physical units are chemical combinations, but the unity is not organic. In living things the unity is much more pervasive, and nevertheless there is greater differentiation in the parts. In a human being the unity is much richer and perfect, but this unity allows for so much distinction within it that the parts can "go their own way" and be in conflict with one another and with the central principle. That is to say, the more perfect the unity, the greater the liberty to the parts and functions, the centripetal and centrifugal tendencies of the two "loves," as it seems, developing apace. Something similar is seen in human institutions, the pack or herd and

* *The Mind and Heart of Love,* pp. 321–322.

slave-owning society passing into one where the unity is most marked and at the same time the members, just by being citizens, are most free. Men and women in society are always looking for a closer unity of friendship and love, which protects and fosters distinction of personality as well as plurality. As Edwin Muir has written: "People have a spring of happiness, not from any privately nursed ideal but simply from the society of friends, an inexhaustible, hidden source." It is, indeed, felt to be an inexhaustible source, one on which Christianity relies, for it teaches that there is a unity of love beyond that known in human society, symbolized in the union of marriage, and realized in that corporate life of which Christ is the Head. The members, rejoicing in the liberty of the sons of God, are animated by divine agape; and this union in turn resembles the supreme one, distantly discerned where three living persons have one Godhead.

Philosophy and experience meet in agreement on the "inexhaustible" worth of personality and mutual love, notwithstanding the difficulty philosophers have in coping with love and persons. By its human constitution the human mind runs to the abstract and general, and this leads philosophers and scientists to a predilection for a mental object, which is too easily made synonymous with spiritual reality. Hence the habit of talking about abstractions like truth and beauty and goodness as if they existed and were somehow superior to the individual and personal. Just because the philosopher dwells among abstractions, "bloodless categories," he is not acclaimed by right in popular estimation as wise, and sometimes loses the credit which is due to him. But even those who are ranked among the perennially wise and are foremost as religious teachers neglect too much the real world where persons live. The reason is that this supposedly real world, especially in past ages, struck them as unhappy and incomplete. *Pereunt et reputantur,* things pass and live only in thought. All is passing, and nothing stays, whereas philosophy and religion look to what is fixed and absolute. "Since the brother of Death daily haunts us with dying Mementoes, and Time that grows old itself bids us hope no long duration, diuturnity is a dream and folly of expectation." But the wrong solution of the undeniable insufficiency of this world is to condemn it as illusion and to take refuge in some ideal and separate world, where persons have no place and meaning. Unless we make the ideal world so alien and inexpressible that it has nothing whatsoever in common or analogous with the present life, it must have its anticipations and presentiments, its symbols and far-off beginnings now; and in fact those who reject the reality of personal life as we know it do draw upon it for illustration, and are bound to do so. They cannot decapitate themselves and then talk; they cannot throw a veil over human love and then excite us about anything we want to hear. Now love is mutual, and persons love one another for what they are. Human life is founded on a plurality of persons. There can be no person in entire isolation, no love and no knowledge. Both family and community are natural units in the sense that we cannot do without them, and the best is drawn out of a child by the influence of an admired or loved personality, whether it be the mother in the home or the outstanding teacher in the school. Persons associate together, and in the company of one another they come to be what they are and taste a unique happiness in the company of friends, in teamwork and in a dangerous task. The laughter and the love of friends, these alone are worth the wear of winning. If death takes them away, then "with a kiss I die." Poetry and art only reflect the desire for love to have a constancy more than mortal, and for lovers to live together. In all religions the favorite images are of the dance or of the song sung in chorus or of supping together or of the marriage feast, and it is the high poet of mysticism, who, in the aftermath of ecstasy, sang:

> Oh night that was my guide!
> Oh darkness dearer than the morning's pride,
> Oh night that joined the lover
> To the beloved bride
> Transfiguring them into each other.*

Christianity differs, therefore, from those religions quoted by Guénon and Aldous Huxley in believing in the "golden string" of personal love which joins heaven and earth. Life, it says, on earth is not illusion, nor can personality disappear in a higher state of union. Without such a defense of human life it is difficult to see how its values can be maintained. Few would deny that Christianity has been the foster mother of Western civilization, and it has performed this function by its constant emphasis on the sacredness of personality. Those for whom God died must by that very act of love possess a worth beyond man's conceiving. We must therefore love one another and live in concord and promote so far as is possible the rights, the independence and the liberties of each individual. Were personality a passing phenomenon we could not love others for themselves, for their intrinsic worth. Another philosophy may say

* From *Poems of St. John of the Cross,* translated by Roy Campbell. Published by Pantheon Books, Inc.

that the divine is hidden in each individual, but such a belief must still leave its holder indifferent to what is illusory in his neighbor, to all, that is, which makes him dear and individual. The God whom the Christians worship is the God of Abraham, Isaac and Jacob, marked individuals and persons, of whom Eric Auerbach has written that they are more real than any Homeric hero. "Time can touch the latter only outwardly, and even that change is brought to our observation as little as possible; whereas the stern hand of God is ever upon the Old Testament figures; he has not only made them once and for all and chosen them, but he continues to work upon them, bends them and kneads them, and, without destroying them in essence, produces from them forms which their youth gave no grounds for anticipating." These men and women have not to lose their personality to be absorbed into a higher reality; they are a chosen people, and in the Christian Good News a new and holy society, *plebs tua sancta,* is to be formed, rejoicing in a new strength and a new love which issues from a divine source. This is to be their plenitude, to become filled with love for one another in a divine family, what St. Cyprian, the African, called in an eloquent phrase, *De unitate Patris et Filii et Spiritus sancti plebs adunata.*

The determining and culminating point of the Christian wisdom is denoted by the presence of personality within the Godhead, love finding its full expression in a way hinted at in the intimacies of human affection, and this Trinity of love creates a world with persons who can respond and be taken up into the rhythm of the divine life. Love is the seal and token of persons, and requires for its ripening liberty and independence. We have only to look on this picture and on another where human personality is but a passing show, to see the difference. In the latter behind the show there is karma or necessity, the everlasting return, and nature is a temporal manifestation or attribute of the Absolute, and man an emanation of the one. Huxley would have us believe that in the Christian religion Jesus Christ should be thought of as an incarnation of divinity like to Krishna and Gotama. He says that in the perennial philosophy there is to be included this doctrine of an Incarnation of the Divine Ground. ". . . Krishna is an Incarnation of the Divine Ground in human form. Similarly, in Christian and Buddhist theology, Jesus and Gotama are Incarnations of divinity," and they serve, as other sages and prophets, as "the best preparation for unitive knowledge." We have not the same well-tested information about Krishna and Gotama as we have about the life of Christ. It appears that Kirshna was one of the manifestations of Vishnu. Unlike Rama, who was a good king, Krishna is said to have been a teacher, whom some identify with the great teacher Vasudeva. Another interpretation, however, would make of Krishna a fertility god. Gotama is recognized to have been an outstanding reformer of Hindu religion, who lived at the same period as Confucius and Pythagoras. He married, taught and died, and his original teaching was in protest against the decadent polytheism current. Deeply sensitive to the misery of life around him he taught the way of abstention and non-existence. From the little that is known of his original doctrine some have asserted that he ignored all theology and that the nirvana he preached is consistent with atheism. It was only long after Gotama's death that what is generally known as Buddhism developed, and the development was affected by the climate of

Hindu theology. In the course of the growth in North India Gotama came to be idealized, after the manner of Krishna, into a manifestation or incarnation of the divine. The word "incarnation" is Huxley's, and it is really quite out of place, and also misleading; whereas "manifestation" is appropriate. In the Buddhist philosophy the world is a passing show, and there is no reason why it should not manifest the face of the divine to enlightened souls. There is nothing incongruous, therefore, in the body of a holy man, or even an animal serving as a preglimpse of the Godhead, and, as Huxley observes, preparing the devout for a fuller vision. Jesus Christ was far from being a manifestation of the divine in this sense. In the New Testament, written within a life's time of his death, he is declared to be God Himself, the divine Son, who took a human nature, body and soul. He is a historical figure, not like Gotama, half real and half mythical, or Krishna, who is in all probability entirely mythical. He is not "the best preparation for unitive knowledge of the Godhead"; if he is the "way," he is also himself the "truth and the life." He does not call this world an illusion; he is the "light of the world." He is to be its "resurrection and life," because his intention is to "give life and that more abundantly"; to breathe a new spirit of love into human persons and invigorate them. Like Gotama he is aware of the misery of man, but this does not lead him to teach the extinction of desire and individuality; instead he bids men to love one another, to bear one another's burdens, and to take up the cross and carry it.

Human love has a regenerative power, and infinitely more so the divine, nor is life on earth such a burden or so encompassed with evil that the only solution is to fly from it. Nor is self the obstacle to union—unless we mean selfishness—for only persons can exchange love. Christ did not teach the extinction of self, but the enhancing of it in a divinely constituted community of which he was to be the head, what the first Christian writer meant when he told his converts to "live the truth in love and so in all things grow up in him, who is the head, even Christ." Karl Marx explained religion as a myth invented to compensate the poor for their hard lot, an unearthly paradise where they would be happy. This idea of religion as a refuge from human life may be justified in part by the teaching of some religions, but Christianity is nearer to the Communist ideal of a perfect society than to the ideal of nirvana or the absorption of the individual in a Divine Ground. As P. de Lubac has said: "Charity has not to become inhuman in order to remain supernatural; like the supernatural itself it can only be understood as incarnate. He who yields to its rule, far from giving up his natural qualities, contributes to those societies of which he is naturally a member an activity that is all the more effective because its motive is more free"; and he quotes P. Marechal, who wrote in his *Studies in the Psychology of the Mystics:* "We understand better that the Catholic mystic is not merely a separated being in comparison with the rest of the faithful, an escapist in search of some hazy transcendence; that the mystic ascent is made up of 'integrations' rather than 'suppressions'; that no specific characterization of the common Christian life should be effaced by it; in short, that the perfect mystic would be as such the perfect Christian, and we mean a Christian whom the highest of divine favours does not withdraw from solidarity in the sufferings and the triumphs of the Church militant."

What then of the alleged likeness, or even identity, between the Christian mystic and those of the other high religions, and what, too, of the place of Christ in the mystic experience? Let us take the second point first. Huxley argues that the mystic experience is at its highest an intuition of or union with the Divine Ground and therefore at a certain stage all thoughts of the Incarnation, that is, in the Christian religion, of Christ himself, must be discarded. The human nature of Christ is finite, whereas the object and end of mystical experience is the infinite reality. The simple answer to this is contained in the words of Christ to Philip that "he that seeth me seeth the Father also," but for its full meaning to be understood the words must be understood in the context of the Last Supper. There Christ prays that these disciples "may all be one, as thou, Father in me, and I in thee; that they also may be one in us; . . . And I have made known thy name to them and will make it known: that the love wherewith thou hast loved me may be in them, and I in them." This passage speaks of the descent of the divine love from the Father to the Son and from the Son to the disciples with the effect that the disciples share in the divine love of the Father for the Son. We can rightly reverse the process and say that the disciples seeing the Son see the Father, that is to say, they are so united by grace and charity to the Son that they can see the Father in him and through him. As we cannot help reading history in the light of our times, and as we see persons and things through the eyes of those we deeply love, so the Christian, but in a much more heightened manner, sees God and life through the eyes of Christ. Grace and love have transformed those chosen to be his friends into a condition in which they say like St. Paul:

"I live, no, no longer I, but Christ lives in me." There is no way to the Father, no sight of Him as He really is, save through His divine image, the Son, and this is the reason why, so far from being an impediment, the Incarnate Son of God is the light and the life whereby we belong to God and enjoy His presence.

However high the state of the individual Christian, other persons are not left behind or in exclusion; they are as much there to the contemplative as the whole orchestra is present to the violinist concentrating on his score. What then of the identity of the language of Christian mystics with that of the Brahmin and the Buddhist, and of what has been called the Highest Common Factor of the high religions, summed up in the words that "it is possible for a man, if he so desires, to identify himself with the spirit and therefore with the Divine Ground, which is of the same or like nature with the spirit"? There are expressions used by Christian mystics, which, if taken literally, would seem to point to identification, and therefore, to some form of pantheism. Tauler writes of the transformation of the soul into God, and as if it were annihilated in the divine being; Eckhart says that there is a mode of union with the Godhead "before He brought forth the Word," and that this is the "summit of Divine Union" when the soul passes into the life of the Godhead; Ruysbroeck uses the expression "the immense sea of divinity" on which the soul sails or into which it plunges; he says, too, that in the essence of God we find *"superessentia nostra,"* our superessence, a condition which transcends all possible human bliss. With this we can compare the descriptions in that medieval English classic *The Cloud of Unknowing* of the union with God "above all substance and knowledge."

Similar statements can be found in many of the other mystics of the great periods, the medieval Flemish and the post-Reformation Spanish. The consensus is too large to be ignored, and it could be paralleled from Islamic mysticism, which Dr. Nicholson says cannot be described "otherwise than pantheistically." Such an interpretation the Moslems are bound to deny, and in the writings of the Christian mystics cited there is almost always an express assertion to be found of the chasm between the finite nature of the creature and God. Eckhart, who is the least orthodox of the Christian company, tells us that "there is no distinction left in the soul's consciousness between itself and God, though God still regards it as a creature." This seems to be a cumbrous way of explaining how the mind of the creature is so lost in the divine loveliness that it has ceased to think of itself at all; and the second part of the sentence corrects any possible misapprehension of the meaning intended. Ruysbroeck insists on the unbridgeable difference between the creator and the creature. Perhaps the most illuminating of all is Tauler in his remark: "I speak not of the reality but of the appearance, the impression that is felt." This suggests that a distinction can be made between what is really happening and the subjective impression of it, as two lovers in the springtime of their passion might talk as if all were shared in their inseparable unity of love.

Any attempt to throw light upon such experiences as the mystics enjoy must be tentative, because the mystics themselves at the end of what they write have to confess that they have been using fallible words. What is remarkable is the agreement amongst the great mystics both as to the nature of the high experience and of the stages which lead to it. That they can talk the same language does make it the more likely that they are, as Tauler says, speaking "not of the reality" so much as "the appearance, the impression that is felt." And this is supported by a problem which arises if we take the descriptions given as a delineation of the reality. That there should be stages, sufficiently well defined, and techniques for advancing in the mystical way, consorts oddly with what we expect from true love. It is as if the soul were exploring some mysterious treasure land or, to use St. Teresa's image, a castle with room after room to be unlocked. The puzzle increases when we reflect that states of mind, not too unlike that of the initial mystic experiences, can be induced by drugs, and moreover that there are many deceits in the way to be avoided and that some of those with mystical gifts have been in no recognizable way saints. Again it is certain that many of the saints, who by their actions prove the depth of their love of God, have not been conspicuous for their mystical experience. Instead of images of climbing stairs or penetrating through room after room of a castle we expect the language of lovers. It is truly there, but not to the exclusion of all else. Now in love there are no exact stages, and when God is the lover, with his grace and his power, he can dispense with all the techniques and processes. No doubt God will adapt his love to the strength and character of each individual person, and in his providence he will work in accordance with human nature. This justifies the idea of process, but it still remains true that in the relation of love there are few or no rules, and God can make a Mary Magdalen forget the world and everything for him in one moment. A logical or semi-scientific account of God in love seems out of place and partly due to a pagan philosophy of an impersonal God.

Where experiences are so exalted as to be beyond any comparison with what we ordinarily know, there is always the danger of misinterpreting them and missing the immense differences which may lie outside the reach of language. Nevertheless on the side of the recipient of them there are clues to follow. It looks as if the recipient were supernormal in the sense that either by disposition or by training and techniques working on the disposition he or she can turn back layers of the self and experience its original pulsations or what has been called the "fine point of the soul." The anima escapes from all the gossip, the information from the forum, the conceptual constructions in which it is educated, its world of appearances, and here in the dark is made aware of its motelike existence in the glow of something much greater. It can call this a source or ground or whole or deity or creator. Deceit is easy here, because the centrifugal tendency of the self is to lose itself in the whole or source. Only the grace of God can set it right. The grace and habit formed from true knowledge have become part of its very nature, and give it a connaturality with the good. The self having shed all that it has is on the ledge of nothingness, an existentialist solo; but, as Heidegger has argued, the Sein is Dasein; there is always a circumambient sea of being in which one is immersed. This sense of belonging can bring an extraordinary sense of death in life, of release from privacy, of the flux and reflux of ordinary events, and of final immersion into an immeasurable ocean of being. But for those whose minds are not lost in the depth the spontaneous reaction is of creature to creator. They feel that they do not belong to themselves, and that their fundamental condition is that of utter dependence on one whose immense majesty fills them with awe, and at times terror. "The beginning of wisdom is the fear of the Lord," and in most of the religions with which we are familiar there is always to be found this dread and reverence for the numinous. Without this awareness of dependence and the infinite distance which separate the creature from the creator worship becomes anthropomorphic, and religious experience a superficial emotion. Awe, however, as religion evolves and God reveals himself in many ways, is warmed by a personal relationship, and grows into love. The "I am who am" becomes the "Father" in the Bible, and the high mystics of all religions begin to vary the pantheistic or monistic teaching with the language of love.

> If you would ask, what is its essence—
> This summit of all sense and knowing:
> It comes from the Divinest Presence—
> The sudden sense of Him outflowing,
> In His great clemency bestowing
> The gift that leaves men knowing naught,
> Yet passing knowledge with their thought.*

The language, nevertheless, of the great mystics of all creeds does bear that resemblance upon which Huxley relies for his belief in the "highest common factor." I have given some reasons why the mystic state should invite such a language. There are also other reasons. One is that the language is very limited which can do justice in any way to the extraordinary experience, and as it has to be in the superlative and in terms of union it is no wonder if there should be an apparent agreement amongst them all. If God is drawing the soul of the true con-

* *Ibid.*

templative to him, the sense of union will be genuine though the language be unrestrained because of the philosophy adopted by the mystic. This is the more likely in that the conscious self is forgotten in an analogous way to that in which we may become unconscious of the presence of our bodies at moments of high concentration of thought. The body is there, and we would not be thinking without it. So too the self is there loving, but "Lost to myself I stayed, My face upon my lover having laid, From all endeavour ceasing." There is another reason, too, why so many of the Christian mystics adopt a language which is not quite the same as that of St. Paul or St. John and bears a likeness, for instance, to that of Neo-Platonism. They thought that they were sitting at the feet of a disciple of St. Paul, Denys the Areopagite—one of the first Christians, therefore, and companion of the Apostles; whereas in fact the writings were those of a Neo-Platonist of the fifth century. He belonged to Alexandria, the meeting place of Jewish, Greek and Christian ideas. After he had been translated into Latin in the ninth century by Scotus Eriugena his influence became very pronounced in early scholasticism when theology and contemplation mingled together, and systematization of thought was in vogue. St. Thomas Aquinas, under the impression that Denys represented the earliest Christian teaching, lent his authority to the works on *The Divine Names* and *The Celestial Hierarchy,* and as a result even the Spanish mystics freely used his terminology and way of approach. There is nothing heterodox in this because the Church was always on the watch to correct any tendencies to pagan ideas, and its watchfulness is seen in its attitude to Eckhart and also to Scotus Eriugena. The main disadvantage has been to embarrass students of the Christian mystics and to give a handle to those who wish to equate mystics of all schools and religions. The ancient philosophies were behindhand in grasping the meaning and role of personality. They were bemused by the vastness of reality, of earth, fire, water and air, by the fugitive and helpless life of man, and by destiny. There is no corresponding word in these ancient languages for what we mean by person. Hence the division between popular religion where gods and goddesses, good and bad abounded, and the uttermost reality which was like to fate, if not something inexpressible. Neo-Platonism contained the idea of the One which was beyond thought and also the hope of passing into it by "ecstasy," an idea much worked upon by the cults which flourished in the Near East, in Egypt and in late Greece. The mysticism which grew under such auspices has its definite marks, and in its pagan form differed greatly from the Jewish and Christian faith. The God of Israel was a living God, and the knowledge of him was an active experience (yada). It was possible to hear God, even if one could not see him. "Be still and know that I am God," where the knowing is a hearing and being brought into touch with God. In the New Testament, as we have seen, a new society of men and women is formed, and in that society of which Christ, the Son of God, is the head, the summit of holiness can be attained. St. Paul was raised to the third and to the seventh heaven; he heard things unspeakable, and he lived co-consciously with Christ. There was no question of a "flight," still less of a "flight from the alone to the Alone." Only the sinners must fly from the face of God, and all earth was meant to be a paradise. The innocent can still at times regain that paradisal contact and be one with the creator in a world of birds and fishes and the lion and the lamb. This mystical tradition is seen in St. Francis of Assisi. Of him Louis Lavelle in his *The Meaning of Holiness* has written truly: "Ozanam calls St. Francis the Orpheus of the Middle Ages. Like Orpheus he tames nature, brings the stones to life, obliges the elements to line up in accordance with the laws of harmony, and brings light to souls that are plunged in darkness, transforming indifference into hope and even anger into love." The point is that in the Bible Adam was intended to be the voice of nature worshiping the creator, and this ideal of the concurrence of inanimate and animate nature as well as the populace of God in a canticle of praise and union with the Trinity belongs to the Christian philosophy, and is embedded in the purpose of the Incarnation and Redemption of Christ. The richness of this ideal shows its face in the Christian liturgy and is drawn upon and remotely expressed in the romanesque and gothic pageantry of symbolic beasts and birds.

With the coming of the writings of the Pseudo-Dionysius and St. Gregory of Nyssa and other Greek Fathers the Neo-Platonic language came into vogue, making the Christian ideal of union with God look more like that of others than is justified. The two conceptions, however, for the reasons already given, worked together. The result, for instance, can be seen in St. Thomas Aquinas, who allows for an experience of a limited kind of the Divine "Ground," but supplements it with his theory of "connaturality." Wisdom, for him, is always intellect fertilized by love, and we see both in his prose and in his poems how personal that relationship of love is and also how communal. As with all the great Christian theologians his first and final word in religion and in the ascent of the soul is *caritas* or *agape*. The proof of this is the affection which the

Christian mystics have had for the Song of Songs. There are commentators who would have us believe that the Song is made up of pastoral love songs, like some of the idylls of Theocritus. Be its origin what it may the lover of God felt that translated to a new key it was the most appropriate of all language for telling what happened to the soul when divine love took possession of it. Hidden meetings, espousals, marriage and the love feast, these are the symbols which suit persons in love, whereas they are out of place if it is question of absorption into a Divine Ground. So far from the mystic fading away into the divine mystery, he or she becomes more and more human and lovable. "May the Lord deliver me," said St. Teresa, "from people who are so spiritual that they wish to turn everything to perfect contemplation, come what may." St. John of the Cross wrote his best poetry round the Song of Songs, and was so in touch with his friends, and his fellow Christians, that he tells us that "he who follows his own individual line of action will be lukewarm in carrying out even things he has learned from God, until he has first communicated them to his fellow men."

The characteristics of Christian mysticism would seem, then, to be these. It strives to keep together, working in harmony, the two fundamental impulses, which I have called centrifugal and centripetal. The first brings the soul to the verge of extinction in a greater reality, and the second helps to keep the poise of the self and to sharpen the mind to intuition. Thus the intellectual and the volitional are kept operative and maintain a balance between the apprehension of the mind and the oblation of the self. But these two impulses are fully in harmony only in the relation of persons, because mutual love is a giving and receiving, "I am his and he is mine," and it is in the Christian religion that persons fill the scene, from the three persons in one God to the creating of human persons, who are both bound in a community and drawn to union with their creator and final end. In the Christian mystic, therefore, the knowledge given by faith seeps into the very substance of the soul and gives meaning and direction in the very experience. It is not a question of a higher and esoteric knowledge arising out of the experience which is independent of and superior to the knowledge of faith. The experience darkens into a pseudo-divine nothingness if it be trusted by itself. But the Christian knows by faith that God is alive and infinitely loving, that the love whereby the soul loves comes from Him and that it is a gift of His grace that the soul should be lifted up into a quasi-equality with the Godhead. Then it can love in Christ, the second Person, with a love which is beyond its own powers, on an equality with the divine lover. Moreover this love comes in and through a community, the society, of which this second Person is the head and animating principle. The heights to which nature can reach we do not know; it would appear that God gives many a contemplative a glimpse through the concentrated vision of the soul of the transcendent, superessential divine beauty. But whatever the heights it can reach it has not the wherewithal to claim an equality with the divine nature. If it does so, as certain mystics seem to claim, then invariably it is lost in the divine immensity, the particle of water is one with the ocean, the coal is consumed in the fire. What is missing in these accounts is the reciprocity of love, that God, too, on his side is an active lover. As a result, one of the chief properties of love is absent, its creative energy, *d'antico amor la gran potenza.* This creativity, as Maritain has shown, is the mark of the poet and the artist who "engender in beauty." Man and woman endow each other with virtue and from their love comes the new birth. This creative power is supremely shown in God's love, who not content with the making of free creatures bestows on them by grace a new life which gives them the power to know and love Him as He is in himself. This love, too, circulates as the blood in the body and so forms a new society, whose name is Agape. So far, therefore, from diminishing personality love exalts it, and it is this life of love, of offering and response, of oblation and plenitude, which defines the Christian ideal.

Of the manner in which this Christian ideal—where wisdom and agape meet—can be fulfilled one illustration will serve. It will save further elaboration and argument. I take it from a résumé by Dr. E. Meissner of the life of a woman named Maria Pilenko. She was a member of a wealthy landowning family in south Russia, and as a student became a revolutionary Socialist. After the Bolshevist Revolution she was shocked by the terrorism which followed it and after denouncing the Communist methods she went into exile in Paris. There she found her way back to religious faith, and straightway set about founding a nunnery, and worked amongst the poor in the worst slums. During the German occupation she gave her time to helping the persecuted Jews, hiding many of them in her convent. Finally she was arrested and sent to the concentration camp at Ravensbruck. I now quote Dr. Meissner. "She had been there for two and a half years when a new block of buildings was erected in the camp, and the prisoners were told that these were to be hot baths. A day came when a few dozen prisoners from the women's quarters were lined up outside the buildings. One girl began to scream. Mother Maria, who had not been selected, came up to her. 'Don't be frightened,' she said, 'look, I will take your turn.' And in line with the rest, she passed through the doors. It was Good Friday, 1945."

Note A

After finishing this chapter I read an article in the July-August, 1954, number of *Blackfriars* by Professor R. C. Zaehner, the Spalding Professor of Eastern Religion and Ethics at Oxford, on "The Menace of Mescalin." He discusses Mr. Aldous Huxley's book, *The Doors of Perception*. In this book Huxley describes the effect upon him of taking the drug mescalin. Before taking it he had never had a mystical experience. The drug, however, enabled him to share, he believes, or counterfeit the experiences which are described by the great mystics of the Eastern religions, Islam and Christianity. With his usual skill Huxley makes us conscious of what happened to him. He first of all found that the world around him was transfigured. "I was not looking now at an unusual flower arrangement. I was seeing what Adam had seen on the morning of his creation —the miracle, moment by moment, of naked existence." On this Zaehner comments: "He was seeing the Dharma-body of the Buddha in the hedge at the bottom of the garden. He was seeing things as they really are." In the next experience time and space cease to be of any importance. His world became "a perpetual present made up of one continually changing apocalypse." The distinction between self and not-self disappeared and Huxley became what he was looking at. At this point Huxley began to feel a lassitude creeping over his will.

"The will suffers a profound change for the worse. The mescalin taker sees no reason for doing anything in particular and finds most of the causes—for which he was prepared to act and suffer, profoundly uninteresting. . . . Thus human beings, unlike flowers and chairs, cease to be of any importance. So far from being transfigured, they are a positive nuisance." As this experience moves on another change occurs, and this time the object seen begins to assume a wonderful but rather terrifying aspect, "wonderful to the point, almost, of being terrifying. And suddenly I had an inkling of what it must feel to be mad." He says that the fear also "was of being overwhelmed, of distintegrating under a pressure of reality greater than a mind, accustomed to living most of the time in a cosy world of symbols, could possibly bear."

Zaehner classifies these experiences as (a) the transfiguration of natural objects into things of unimaginable beauty, (b) the feeling that one sees things transfigured and *is* them, and (c) the sudden panic when the vision seems too overpoweringly real to face. His comments on them are full of interest, and I quote them or synopsize them. The first is certainly not what in one place Huxley claims as an experience of the Beatific Vision. "What he seems to have seen . . . was a part of creation as God sees it, or he saw maya in individuation as thought by Brahman, not as normally seen by men." It "bears a striking resemblance to what the Zen Buddhists call satori, and Huxley tends to use Zen language for it. The drug served as a short cut for what is attained usually by long Zen discipline." The second experience is of identity, what the Mahayana Buddhists mean by saying, "Nirvana is samsara." All living becomes unimportant; the "transformed person is beyond good and evil, which, like time and space, have only relative value. He has become like a god, and he is deliriously happy in his sense of identity with nature." If we accept the collective unconscious of Jung, then human consciousness is like the part of an iceberg which is visible, the personal unconscious is the submerged part, and the collective unconscious is the sea from which it draws its being. This collective unconscious is neutral, neither good nor bad, and "like the prakriti of the Samkhya system, it can either help or hinder the development of the 'self' which is the term used by Jung to mean the integrated personality." In this second experience Huxley with the help of mescalin has entered into communion with this collective unconscious and cut himself off from the conscious and voluntary self. Jung has often met this case and seen as a result incipient madness. This analysis is confirmed by the next stage of Huxley's experience. But can this experience of identity be called in any sense an identity with God or the "Divine Ground"? "Huxley has merely confused the issue by chattering glibly about the Beatific Vision, Sat Chit Ananda and the rest. It is not enough to talk about an experience of identity. The question is: identity with what?" Zaehner holds that Huxley has confused so-called pantheism, monism and monotheism, whereas there is all the difference in the world between them; he has also confused natural mysticism and theistic mysticism. The natural mystic "feels himself to be identical with the outside world—in Rimbaud's words, he becomes 'a fabulous opera.'" There is a danger in identifying oneself with nature; it means dissociation between the conscious self and the will and the dark, subterranean world of the unconscious; it means, too, calling creatures by the name God, and the consequence of this is fear which is near to panic and madness.

I quote this criticism of Professor Raehner both for its intrinsic interest and because it supports on so many points the view developed in the text. Mescalin brings out the subjective element in mystical experience without necessarily invalidating its testimony. The experience, according to Raehner covers both natural and montheistic mysticism. I should prefer to say that the natural, the God-given and the supernatural may all be present together, and this is why wise direction is so essential. The purely natural and counterfeit experience is seen in the effect of certain drugs which stimulate the human system and produce an intense vision like that, for instance, of Rimbaud. This intense experience leads on to the identification of the self with nature and reality. To explain this Raehner calls upon the "collective unconscious" of Jung, and I do the same. There are also other possible explanations of the phenomenon. Miss Jacquetta Hawkes suggests that in some way living nature is immanent in us, in what she calls the "old brain" in distinction to our more immediate and present consciousness which belongs to the "new brain." "Let anyone who wishes really to grasp and accept the continuity of life hold out his hand, look at it with unaccustomed eyes, feel its bones and nails, and see if, from somewhere at the base of memory, he cannot recover the feeling of the dark, warm mud squeezing between scaly claws." The "warm dark mud" in the view I touch on in the text and developed more fully in *The Mind and Heart of Love* expresses that feeling of loss in the dark when the anima, that is the centrifugal urge of the self, abandons itself without regard to or protection from the animus, the counterbalancing urge. This explanation is borne out by what happens after the experience of identity in Huxley's account. He says that the will suffers a profound change for the worse and ceases to be interested in persons or in any of the duties or ideals of ordinary life. In other words, the animus, the self which seeks to maintain and develop its personality, is always in danger from the siren voices which call it to self-surrender, and this is a temptation from within and never can be overcome completely save by the loving presence of another Person. In the Christian religion, as Zaehner points out, the oblation of the self to a loving God rights the balance and the self is not destroyed but elevated into the society of three Persons in one God. But just because drugs and psychopathical causes can ape the genuine mystical state, there is no reason for denying the genuine experience and the influence of grace upon the soul. As God works through ordinary experience in the conferring of grace, so the intense psychosomatic conditions are not incompatible with divine communion. For those who have eyes to see there is an immense difference between the statements of the great mystics of the East and the conditions described by Huxley. One excellent test offered by Friedrich von Hügel is the expansion or contraction of personality and love. The psychopathic loses interest in his duties and in his friends, and becomes more and more self-centered; the genuine mystic becomes more and more generous and integrated. The Eastern is full of pity and the Christian of love, and we cannot put a term to the intimacy with which God converses with them. What also emerges, however, from Huxley's account is the importance of a controlling and directing philosophy. Knowledge is essential where, as we have seen, the private experience can become so engrossing and bewitching.

In the light of this experiment of Huxley's and much other evidence, I suggest that there are at least three forms of mystical experience: one which can be called nature mysticism, a second, solitary mysticism, and the third, Christian. The first is indicated, probably in the psychologists' language of the return to the womb, for instance in the Magna Mater worship. The second is a mode of stripping of self so as to procure an experience which is ineffable and felt to be identification with what is supreme and perfect. The third is the Christian, based on knowledge and love, which moves in the circuit of persons and personal love.

IV.

The Divine Union and the Self

DR. ANANDA COOMARASWAMY had the noble ambition of bringing the East and West together under one spiritual and philosophical ideal, and Mr. Aldous Huxley makes an, at first sight, attractive case for his version of perennial wisdom. If the plea be unsuccessful, the wealth and beauty nevertheless of the religious ideas which he and others of his school have brought together are undeniable. Presented with such a testimony to the high spirit of man, gathered from all ages and from East and West, an unprejudiced mind must feel downcast in the presence of many of the alternatives offered today, be they Marxist, bourgeois, existential or empiricist. Whatever be the difference manifested on a close inspection of the evidence gathered together, that evidence cannot be put aside as romantic or abnormal. It is too massive and too constant; it exhibits a common trait and one indelible characteristic, the surge of the mind and heart to discover a ladder of perfection. Those too who follow this way are convinced that they have found the principle of peace and unity in a world of disorder and anxiety.

The outward look of the various religions from which Mr.

Aldous Huxley has drawn his texts in *The Perennial Philosophy* and the language differ, as he admits; the message, however, to his mind, is the same. "The vestments, as Plutarch said, are variegated to represent the cosmos; that of Osiris is white, symbolizing the Intelligible Light beyond the cosmos!" Let us say that it is not so much Osiris as the Intelligible Light which unites Plutarch and the Buddhist and the Hindu. Now, as we have seen, wisdom has been thought of as a quick or loving discernment, as a form of synthetic apprehension, or as a mode of mystical experience beyond all seeing and telling. The quotations given by Mr. Huxley, whether they be from the Upanishads, the Tibetan Book of the Dead, *The Cloud of Unknowing,* William Law or St. Teresa, agree on the necessity of self-knowledge, the purification of the senses, and a hidden quality in supreme perfection, which has to be sought with the whole mind and will. Equally it has to be admitted that there is within this agreement a differing point of view, often made explicit, about the nature of the Deity, the permanent value of human life, both of soul and body, and the character and importance of the mystical experience. To take one text as an example. In the Tantra Tattva we are told that "in the root divine wisdom is all-Brahman; in the stone she is all-Illusion; in the flower she is all-World; and in the fruit, all-Liberation." The emphasis on this world of ours is different in this text from, for instance, that of the Jewish or Christian philosophy, as different as the effect of light upon a sundial and on the ark of the covenant. It is hard, at first sight, to see how such a view leaves any promise of succor to a world in distress. *Mentem mortalia tangunt,* and a reader of one of the stories told in the Pali scriptures may well be as much disconcerted as edified. The story is that the Brahman Drona, seeing the Blessed one sitting at the foot of the tree, asked him, "Are you a deva?" And the Exalted One answered, "I am not." "Are you a gandharva?" "I am not." "Are you a yaksha?" "I am not." "Are you a man?" "I am not a man." On the Brahman asking what he might be, the Blessed One replied, "Those evil influences, those cravings, whose non-destruction would have individualized me as a deva, a gandharva, a yaksha, [three types of supernatural being], or a man, I have completely annihilated. Know therefore that I am Buddha."

If this explanation of the Blessed One were to be taken literally, it would imply that all states, human and super-human, are as passing shows. As always, however, in such statements we must allow for a certain extravagance. In order to impress upon the novice the incomparable perfection to be sought and the need of an uncompromising dedication to it the teacher has to use the language of "all or nothing." At the same time neither the Hindu nor the Buddhist troubles to safe-guard finite perfection and human values in the same way as the Jewish and Christian philosophies. Again the mystical experience is put as the be-all and end-all of human effort, whereas in much Protestant theology mysticism is regarded as an intruder, and in Catholic teaching it is aligned with charity and intellectual belief. This does not mean, however, that we are rendered incapable of asking questions about the nature of the Hindu kindred ideals, or of comparing them with the Christian. There is an abundance of material, philosophic and theological, in the Eastern commentaries, and it is this wisdom which can be studied and set side by side with that of the Near East and the West. We have to ignore to some extent, it is true, the distinction between the metaphysical and the mystical tradition which in certain contexts would be important. But so long as we do not think of this metaphysical tradition as a purely philosophic one, all is well, and the word "wisdom" carries with it a sense beyond the merely philosophical. Sankara, Solomon, Socrates, Dionysius and Aquinas meet together under the shadow of its wings. Moreover the word *wisdom* gives a framework for discussion which can be understood by all. Though wide in its reference it has, unlike the word *prudence,* retained its traditional meaning. It is still used as a term of respect, and everyone likes to be thought wise in some degree. Those who are contrasted with the wise are spoken of as superficial or clever or narrow-minded or erudite. "Learning comes but wisdom lingers." Everyone, so it is believed, can make something of his experience; the sailor knows the signs of the sky and the way ships behave; the countryman knows the soil and the habits of the livestock he tends. Doctors, lawyers and statesmen, too, can develop a sixth sense, which people trust. In fact the public craves for oracles though it does not always look in the right place. It does not, for instance, turn too readily to the professional philosopher, the class, that is, of those who by their very name should be fond of wisdom. The reason for this may be that it has been so often disappointed. Philosophy has its heroes and its saints, but also its simpletons and sophists.

The great age of speculation in Greece ended in the dry sands of cynicism, and the history of philosophy in the last three hundred years has been checkered. The failures of the gigantic attempts of the German idealists have brought ambitious speculation into disrepute, and more and more university teachers have restricted themselves to criticizing the instrument of thought and improving the logic of statements. The present age is doubtful of its own foundations and almost buried under the problems which have fallen upon it. Among scientists the dogmatism of the nineteenth century has collapsed with the breakdown of the Newtonian physics and the discovery of ugly little facts which destroy the most beautiful of theories. The theorists stand at the moment empty handed, and are anxious to make terms with the technologists and engineers. This negative attitude, in so far as it means the abandonment of a materialistic metaphysics, may be a step toward a true philosophy of nature, and it is also beneficial in that it leaves the specialist to cultivate his own garden and abound in good sense there without distractions. Unfortunately, however, a certain type of scientist is drawn to philosophy as the moth to the candle. Nor is this surprising after all; the philosopher has often written much nonsense about science. The matter we study, and the manner in which we study it, unconsciously take a hold upon us; the energy of nature must be the energy of man and the energy of spirit; the contents of the water in the tumbler must be a microcosm of the universe. Hence we extend the regulating principles, the methods of our particular science, and the concepts appropriate to it, to other regions of reality, as if they were of the same order. The living and non-living are set together, brain and thought are identified, and the empirical thinker measures with his yardstick the spiritual and the metaphysical. In so doing each fails to notice the limitations which he has voluntarily imposed upon himself in the special branch of science which is his own. When first the physical scientists discovered the immense gain accruing to them from the application of physico-mathematical methods, they were conscious that they were prescinding from other aspects of reality. In time, however, as the old metaphysic was forgotten and the new methods proved startlingly successful, they assumed that they had the means of knowing everything intelligible in the universe. It was as if in a ten-cent store the fixing of one price made all the goods alike in every respect. For this reason the reminder given by Mr. Austin Farrer in his *The Glass of Vision* is so salutary. "The sciences yield real information about the world, but only in terms of the conceptual instruments. It is only the relation of real things or events to the instruments that is disclosed; it is only the relation of the size of things to a yard-measure which is discovered by the use of a yard-measure, and only the relation of the structure of real processes to the formulated pattern of causal uniformity, which is discovered by the use of causal uniformity. . . . The true scientist is justly credited with a supreme respect for fact, that is to say, the real world upon which he makes his experiments. He will stubbornly refuse to record what his yardstick does not bring to light, or to construct in defiance of any least thing that it does. This is rightly called respect for fact; but it can scarcely be called respect for being."

Because of the limitation the scientist imposes on himself in his inquiry he is the aide-de-camp and standby of the wise man, unless of course he reaches beyond his particular study to a general conspectus of the universe and man. He is one of the team whose names at the beginning of a film precede that of the principal director. The philosophical mind is, as we have seen, the one which is supposed to have this office. He puts aside his yardsticks, and, as Mr. Farrer says, looks at "being in its whole range and in all its dimensions." For this he must keep in touch with facts and be ready to fall back upon them, but solely that he may know better the ultimate nature of things, how and why the experiences of man are what they are. The scientist assumes the world of sensible appearance and divides it up into separate departments such as the physical, the chemical, the electronic and the biological; he takes man and makes statistical surveys of his acts, treats of him as an economic unit or in terms of institutions. It is for the philosopher to ask what is space and what is time, what is the nature which allows it to change and pass from one form to another; what again is the nature of man, that paradoxical figure, a part of nature and yet able to stand aside from it and reason about it, self-conscious and yet so ignorant of himself, and described at various times as a thinking reed, a tool-bearing animal and a son of God. Descartes, the father of modern philosophy, identified philosophy with the pursuit of wisdom and described it as "the knowledge of truth by its first causes." He and most other philosophers made it their task to find order in the universe, not an arbitrary nor convenient one, but an order intrinsic to it and governed by ultimate causes. To find such an order was the aim of Plato and Aristotle, and it is resumed by Aquinas when he defined philosophy as the science which considers first and universal causes; "wisdom considers the first causes of all causes" (in Metaph. I, lect. i.).

In such a pursuit there is no self-imposed limitation, no yardstick as in the empirical sciences. "The final joy of man consists in the superlative activity of his supreme power, truth" (Opusc. X de Causis, Lect. I). If there be any limita-namely the activity of mind engaged with incomparable tion in philosophic thinking it must be due not to any self-denying ordinance but to an imperfection inherent in human thinking. The extreme rationalist regards such a suggestion as obscurantist, the skeptic and cynic think that it is only too obvious that the mind deceives and that truth is a mirage. The constant reiteration of one or other of these extremes shows the presence of some weakness, and this conclusion is confirmed by the language drawn from human experience. The principal Eastern philosophies start from the premise of self-delusion, and all forms of idealism depend for their argument on the antinomies of ordinary experience. The point of Kant's *Critique of Pure Reason* rests on the inadequacy of the human mind to make intelligible statements about reality as it is in itself. Our human mind sees reality according to its own structure and therefore imposes its own forms and ways of seeing on what is presented to it in experiences. In this Kant diverged from the more traditional view which has kept to a middle way; this, while acknowledging the limitations of human thought and a modicum of self-ignorance, believes that the mind of man is capable of truth and is a humble pupil of wisdom.

So much has been expected from philosophy that to many its achievements have appeared very disappointing. They must think it scandalous that a pursuit followed by the keenest of intellects and dedicated to truth should be a tale of continual controversy, ambitious error and clues leading nowhere. A view which is all persuasive to one generation is discarded by the next; and many a name passes from fame to infamy, to be a butt for textbook writers. There is no denying that the oddest of views enliven the somewhat dull pages of philosophic history, and that in retrospect many a theory looks malformed or undersized and does little more than represent the prejudices and assumptions of the age in which it was conceived. Much can be written against the pretensions of the philosophers. Nevertheless it is possible to detect a voice of wisdom amid the babel of contention and contradiction, a voice which is distinct and grows in strength with time. It does not depart from good sense, but as it stretches out it gathers more and more into its song, until, as it seems, it is reaching from end to end and passing into a divine word. There is a semblance of a law in the growth of philosophical knowledge, unlike the law of scientific progress. Theories come and go, and many of them lie dead; others revive under different forms. But wherever there has been serious thought something survives, an idea or aspect or even a detail, the point of which had not previously been properly appreciated. A view crumbles to dust, and in the dust is a small piece of truth. That is why it is unwise to neglect the thinkers of the past, even though we may disagree with them on what they themselves think to be most important.

In former ages philosophy and religion were intimately connected, and theology was held to be the queen of the sciences. Since the advent of the scientific age this connection has been broken. True, a great scientist like Newton had strong religious beliefs, and leading philosophers like Leibniz, Berkeley, and Hegel made God the center of their systems. But the empiricist tradition, taking its cue from the methods of the scientists, has disposed of the matter and almost standardized a separation of religion and philosophy, like that of church and state. The information, now widely diffused, about the Eastern philosophies may, perhaps, help in time to restore the alliance. They supply further evidence of the intimate connection between metaphysics and religion, for, while keeping their own autonomy, they borrow light from each other. The evidence for this is overwhelming. Greek and Arabian thinkers, the Neo-Platonists, the medieval scholastics, Descartes, Malebranche, Berkeley, the German idealists, Bergson and Whitehead in their later days, these and others cover the great periods of Western civilization; and now we can scan the history of China and India and Japan and observe the mutual regard of religions and philosophy. At times indeed the God of philosophy and the God whom men worship draw apart, because thought robs of its singularity what it touches; but as thinking is the act of man and not of the mind by itself, once he starts thinking on the ultimate meaning of the world and of himself, his speculation is bound to terminate at "the ground of being" or at "I am who am." The alternative—and it is one which makes an appeal now—is to dismiss all speculation of this kind as spurious, as a wild-goose chase. Metaphysical statements are platitudes or unverifiable or emotional noises. They are the bubbles which appear when the mind is overheated.

This is not the place to challenge the modern attack upon metaphysics. It is here assumed that what for ages has been called wisdom is not a meaningless word, and that the reverence and cult of it in past civilizations is not due to a confusion of emotion with reason. "Ever," as the Book of Wisdom declares, does "the gracious, ordering of wisdom" manifest itself. "She from my youth up has been my heart's true love." Both in the intellectual and in the moral order the uncertainty caused by confusion is our *bête noire;* peace, in Augustine's definition, is the tranquillity of order, as anxiety and delirium are the products of disorder. A contemplative soul, like Dame Juliana of Norwich, enjoys the most perfect peace humanly possible because she is given to understand in a vision the divine providence. All is well and everything has a meaning. "See I lead all things to the end I ordained at the beginning by the same Might, Wisdom and Love whereby I made them. How could anything be amiss?" Those, on the other hand, who are not so privileged are tormented precisely because of the apparent waste of what is good, precious and promising. The opposition between individual life and the human theories of it is the theme of Kierkegaard and the existentialists as of the patient in the clinic. "Beauty is but a flower which wrinkles will devour." *Animula, vagula, blandula, quo nunc abibis in loca?* These are the besetting questions which circle around human life and cry out for an answer. The rationalist systems make all smooth and logical, and therefore arouse only an irritation against philosophy. The empiricist acknowledges evil, but disclaims any responsibility on his part to provide answers. In so far as neither keeps company with religion, like Icarus their wings melt and they fall to earth. They do not possess the wisdom with which the ancient philosopher was credited.

In place of "the ancient philosopher," it would be better to write "the perennially wise" in the sense intended by Guénon and Huxley and Coomaraswamy. These are the philosophers who start from the predicament in which man finds himself and seek for ultimate explanations of this plight and of man's destiny. Their explanations differ, and, therefore, if there be any perennial truth, from them it will have to be extracted.

Religious metaphysics, however, has also had its ups and downs. The perennial philosophers, of the type of Mr. Huxley, believe that they can extract from the various versions a common and enduring truth, but this kind of philosophizing seems to suffer from certain defects. The human mind does not seem to be at ease either with the purely sensible or the purely spiritual. It cannot even conceive of the spiritual without the help of a sensible symbol or sign. The words we use to describe the immaterial show traces of their origin in the material. But when we come to the material, it is the mind which is the troublesome partner. It cannot take in the individual. We all know how difficult it is to communicate a private experience to another person; we have to keep adding details, and we add similes and analogies in the hope that he will realize what the experience was like. It is easier when we write or speak of the objects of our senses, because they are public. Nevertheless the human mind strips them of their individuality, and then out of the disembodied forms proceeds to make a coherent logical pattern. Our philosophical formulations, as a consequence, tend to be lifeless, as inhuman and as necessitated as a geometrical system. The religious mind feels very ill at ease with these abstractions and takes refuge in a non-rational faith or in a mystical experience or in a general denial of the relevance of theology to religious experience. Moreover the form conceived by the mind, be it a subject or attribute, takes on the look of a thing in itself, existing by its own warrant; and these substantiated essences are the occasion of much loose thinking and nonsense. We make friends with Adversity, trust our Luck, and talk glibly of mankind, democracy, the general will, relativity and even wisdom.

The modern logicians have exposed as never before the many errors into which language, especially the language of emotion, can lead us. This onslaught has destroyed many of the weeds which grew in the more pretentious systems of meta-physics. For their work of demolition and disrespect for the past these logicians have been viewed by the conservative-minded with apprehension and dislike. The first essays of these logical iconoclasts merited criticism, if not dislike, because their destructive powers were directed to the overturning of all of the old tables of the law, in ethics and religion as well as in metaphysics. The first impiety has, however, been succeeded by a painstaking and thorough overhauling of traditional logic and language, and as so often happens, in philosophy as well as in painting and poetry, part of what at first shocked is made welcome, domesticated and ends by being a perennial pos-session. What makes, however, many exasperated in the present debate is the feeling that never have the times been so out of joint, and that the contribution of the philosophers is not serious. Here at the moment when the civil authorities are pre-paring the population in protective measures against nuclear attack the wise men are fiddling. Those who voice this senti-ment complain of a *trahison des clercs,* the absence of any sav-ing truth in the work of contemporary scientists, poets and philosophers and religious thinkers. But if truth does not ride in at the crack of a showman's whip, it is all the same not invisible nor idle. The worst that can be said is that it is not properly dressed for the part; it wears old clothes which it keeps admiring and is indifferent to changing fashions. The wise man need not dress like a pantaloon. Truth can never be entirely hidden; it is the good fortune of every man to become acquainted with it, but it is more easily recognizable in clothes suited to present needs. If we examine the so-called perennial wisdom in its development in the past, one special feature is unmistakable, and that is its power to separate off from the passing ideas and mood of a generation, the excesses of prejudice and the overstatements and the understatements, what is fresh and lasting. It is a coat of many colors. True knowledge does not change its face; it is not a contemporary hypothesis serving as a make-belief until with new facts a better one is constructed. It remains ever the same, but as Mr. Eliot has said of a great poem, it is forever becoming more alive as readers make fresh discoveries in its inexhaustible subject matter. Whereas what a scholar learned at a medical school in ancient Alexandria or at Bologna in the Middle Ages is of only antiquarian interest to the medical faculty of the Mayo Institute or Guy's Hospital, the learning of the Platonic Academy, of the Lyceum, of Socrates and Epictetus, Plotinus, Denys and Duns Scotus still educates the mind. What is false drops away, and the remainder increases the permanent capital of human wisdom. There is then a slow and natural process of increase, accelerated at times by the outstanding genius of individuals and delayed by the bitterness of controversy, which, in turn, exaggerates the differences separating the contending parties. At times, it must be owned, it is difficult to discern anything of value in a new movement—the dadaist or surrealist, for instance; but then new views, especially when they run contrary to our dearly held convictions, are instinctively resisted and condemned *en bloc*. We do not pause to remember that a new and challenging set of ideas is often a reflection and crystallization of the spirit and wants of an age, the barometer or sensitive conscience, exaggerated and partial, of something wrong or neglected. Innovators are the dissatisfied strikers protesting against our management of the world's spiritual funds; and there are many of us more concerned with protecting our own dignity than in extending our vision and joining together what has fallen asunder. The new universe floated by the scientists drifts away into a black cloud; the world of art becomes a private dream, and statesmen have to compound with slavery. It is not enough just to complain that one group of modern philosophers spends its time sharpening the language of communication, that another group is "committing itself" in an absurd world, proud in its anguish and holding fiercely to its one last possession, the will; while a third is summoning the underground forces of the self to the world's aid. The part of wisdom is constantly to dress our days as they come to "a dexterous and starlight order," and to do this it is necessary to appreciate and reassemble what is thrown up or strewed about in the world around us. The Victorians took for granted that only certain subjects were fit material for art. They were wrong, as the geniuses of modern art have proved. There are those who wring their hands and prophesy that nothing but disaster can follow from the way society is drifting. To refuse to share in these jeremiads does not mean compromise with evil nor a false optimism. Those who belong to an ancient tradition may be the most fixed in their convictions; but they know what is in human nature and are not so alarmed at setbacks as the romantic or the progressive. They look beyond the present and rely upon the grace of God.

In the development of the Western philosophy the wise have time and again borrowed from what first appeared alien and even hostile. The Bible gives an outstanding example in the Sapiential Books, where the Greek influence is unmistakable. But while many passages are redolent of Neo-Platonism, the accent remains Jewish, and the wisdom which is praised is more the breath of a living God, condensed, for example, in the Law, than a subsistent Platonic essence. Again, the early Christian thinkers took freely from the metaphysical language of the Greek philosophers, and in the formulation of human and divine law made use of the Stoic ideas of nature and virtue. Anders Nygren has argued that this borrowing infected the pure doctrine of the Gospels, but as we owe to it the reign of law, of moral custom and most of the permanent institutions of Western civilization, our attitude should be one of gratitude for the open-mindedness of the early Church. Those times are now so distant that we fail to realize the courage and vision needed to pick out and incorporate what was fair in the contending pagan philosophies of the time. They could have stopped short when they saw that to Socrates virtue was knowledge and sin nothing more than ignorance, that Aristotle gave no place to the creative activity and wrote ambiguously on the nature of the soul, that the Stoics identified God with nature and necessity. Instead, as Newman has written, the Church from the first "looked round upon the earth, noting and visiting the doctrines she found there. She began in Chaldea, and then sojourned among the Canaanites, and went down into Egypt, and thence passed to Arabia, till she rested in her own land. Next she encountered the merchants of Tyre, and the wisdom of the East country, and the luxury of Sheba. Then she was carried away to Babylon, and wandered to the schools of Greece. And wherever she went, in trouble or in triumph, still she was a living spirit, the mind and voice of the Most High; 'sitting in the midst of the doctors, both hearing them and asking them questions'; claiming to herself what they said rightly, correcting their errors, supplying their defects, completing their beginnings, expanding their surmises, and thus gradually by means of them enlarging the range and refining the sense of her own teaching."

This "looking round the earth, noting and visiting the doctrines she found there," was carried out in the first contacts of the Christian missionaries with the Chinese and Hindu cultures after the Middle Ages. Men like Ricci in China and Robert de Nobili in India were ready to admire what they found and wished to absorb what was best, in so far as it was compatible, with the wisdom they had learned. A still better opportunity now is offered, as the abundant literature of and on the Hindu and Buddhist scriptures lies open before us. In a world which is distressed and lacks any acknowledged directing philosophy of life the Eastern sages remind us of the need of meditation, self-discipline and tranquillity of mind. With the specter of *1984* haunting us, it is not easy to possess the soul in peace. The world has become alien and hostile; "western man has moved across a Rubicon which, if as unseen as the 38th Parallel, seems to have been as definitive as the Styx." The break with the past described in these words of Mr. David Jones is far from bringing us into a promised land. He himself hints at a world of "estrangement and misunderstanding," where there is "a radical incompatibility" between the world of the "myths" and the world of the "formulae"; in fact a no-man's land. Maladjustments, compensation, split personality, the language of the psychiatrist has entered into common speech, and misfits multiply. Men and women in the midst of plenty are losing their identity. They can no longer, in Yeats' phrase, "hold reality and justice in a single thought"; nor can they with the Christian poet kiss their hands to the stars, "lovely-asunder starlight, wafting him out of it," nor see him "under the world's splendor and wonder." Modern education does much to inform and enlighten the mind, but it is ill-equipped to provide co-ordinating principles and an ideal of unity. A hundred years ago Nietzsche was denouncing the learned for being no more than "wandering encyclopaedias"; what the young learned from them "did not complete nature; it only kills your own nature." A teaching which has no point and gives no direction leaves an aching void which has to be filled, and one of the reasons often given for the influence of Marxism upon the educated is that it is a creed with a mission and puts destiny into the hands of the young.

Wisdom is the art of co-ordinating our multiple experience and bringing order into chaos. "She reacheth from end to end mightily and ordereth all things sweetly." To the writer of these words the universe was a smaller cosmos than what we know now, and he was not vexed with the kinds of doubts and uncertainties which have multiplied with the enormous extension of information in modern times. Solomon, the model of the wise man to the Israelites, was not a "wandering encyclopaedia." He knew the signs of the zodiac, lakes and the near Mediterranean Sea, mountains and valleys, beasts and birds. Above all he knew the God of Abraham, Isaac and Jacob, and what was in man. These sufficed, and despite all the new knowledge that has come, modern man looks out on a world of space and time and fellow beings who have the same virtues and vices, the same desires and frustrations, the same sorrows and joys as Solomon. Science has its Copernican revolutions, and there is little in common between the hypotheses of a Roger Bacon and an Einstein, the atoms of Lucretius and of Lord Rutherford. Philosophy changes, and it is beholden to science, especially in certain branches, such as psychology and cosmology, but it is maintained by those human experiences, which vary in degree and not in kind and are the prerogative of every man, whether he live in a cave or a skyscraper. What David Jones says of the artist is true in its degree also of the philosopher: "there is only one tale to tell even though the telling is patient of endless development and ingenuity and can take on a million variant forms. I imagine something of this sort to be implicit in what Picasso is reported as saying: 'I do not seek. I find.' " Those who live now have a heightened sensibility; they have come to appreciate and cherish what was present always but not realized: freedom, the rights of the individual and the impartiality of the mind required in the assessment of evidence. Science has filled in many of the gaps which in earlier days led philosophers to jump to hasty conclusions. Aristotle could talk nonsense about the celestial bodies, Descartes about the function of the pineal gland, Berkeley about the efficacy of tar water. We are slower now to assign causes in nature and to attribute to the mind many of those intermediate activities called psychophysical. The modern world is saved many of the mistakes of the past, and it is also dumbfounded and alarmed by the rise of new problems, ethical, political, scientific and private. It does not fall to the philosopher to supply ready answers to the infinitely varied questions which can be asked. Encyclopedias, reference books and specialists are with us to serve that need. What these cannot do is provide a tranquillity of order, the theme which creates and unites the motifs of a culture. Where there is no theme the individual is left in a confusion which begets a heart-ache as well as a headache. He feels at the mercy of events, which it is his duty to bestride, and he has no inkling of any design in the events which crowd his life. Anger and despair are declared by Sartre to be the notes of our epoch. "Ours," says Malraux, "is the first civilisation searching for man which does not understand itself." But this is an exaggeration. Melancholy pervades the Greek Anthology, and despair appears often on Roman inscriptions. The Marxist explanation of religion as the mythical compensation for human misery has this of truth in it, that men have always been shadowed by anxiety, and the religious philosophies of East and West have offered a means of salvation from it. The means have differed and have included resignation to fate, a law of justice with reward and punishment, a final vindication or triumph, or a release from error and illusion and an ultimate union with nirvana.

According to the nature of the answer will be the shaping now of things to be, the metaphysical scheme, that is, and the place of the self, soul and body, in it. The aim of the Gnostic and the Eastern philosophies alike is so to purify the self and elevate the mind that the values of the temporal and divided world dwindle to nothingness. They are other-worldly. In the West the opposite tendency reaches its culmination in the Hegelian synthesis. Here the transcendent but abstract ideal is embodied in nature and history; it overcomes the apparent estrangement between object and subject, nature and thought, humanity and God, in a dialectical process, not yet fully completed. The city of Kekrops becomes the city of God. The Christian philosophy strives to hold a balance between these two tendencies; it places ultimate perfection in a life above and beyond time, which consists in an endless love between God and man. At the same time it conserves the values of the temporal and finite. Such a summary cannot of course do justice to the many and subtle qualifications which bring these religions closer or further apart, and each must finally be judged on its logic and its fidelity to experience as well as by the intrinsic perfection of the ideal it sets forth. The Hindu reproaches the Christian with being still imprisoned in time and with making an idol out of what is finite. The Christian replies that "everlasting life" begins now, that the finite is not an illusion and can keep its tender and subsistent being in coexistence with what is one and infinitely perfect—and that it is better so. "He taketh not away our mortal joys who giveth heavenly life," as the Epiphany hymn asserts. To resign all human values is to make a solitude and call it peace.

A philosophy worthy of the name must be a coherent system or whole, and the same holds true of religion. The richer, too, and more inclusive the unity the more likely is it to be the ideal sought after. Hence the number and importance of its omissions can serve as a useful preliminary test of a system claiming to be true. Materialism and idealism can both be criticized on this count for underestimating one side of human experience. The sensitive spots in a religious philosophy are to be found especially in the relationship of the infinitely perfect to the imperfect, and secondly in the treatment of the status and suffering of that imperfect being man. The spiritual writings of both West and East emphasize the relative nothingness of man. "He, the self is to be described by no, no!" and, "What is man that Thou are mindful of him?"

They are equally insistent on what Pascal calls "la misère de l'homme." Suffering and error are the bane of secular philosophers, the weed in their trim and contrived gardens. Myth finds a way out, and the beast can turn into beauty. The religious thinker dwells long on suffering. Sin brings suffering and suffering brings wisdom is the refrain of Aeschylus and other ancient dramatists. They are not all, however, equally prepared to admit suffering into the heart of the religious mystery. Christian Science encourages us to believe that it is nonexistent. Epicurus, though he held that without suffering man would have no motive to learn about nature, set as the end and object of all learning and desire the avoidance of pain. Cleanthes, the Stoic, taught resignation with the belief that all is well; evil fits in with good "into one great whole, so that in all things reigns one reason everlastingly." Sufferings, therefore, are to be treated like troublesome insects: to be brushed aside if possible, or else to be used to strengthen the self's inner life. Whatever happens, that inner composure, so in accordance with universal reason, must not be disturbed.

The Buddhist sage, as befits a religion which began from the compassion aroused at the sight of human misery, begins with the lesson of suffering; "decay is inherent in all component things." The Four Noble Truths sum up the teaching. "The elements which make up man produce a capacity for pain. The cause of pain is the craving for individual life. Deliverance from craving does away with pain. The way of deliverance is the Eightfold Path." In other words, suffering is the prevailing condition of human life, and this makes life worthless and unhappy. The cause of this is the desire for worldly pleasures and pursuits and an attachment to them.

There is no way out along this line, for it means endless repetition of birth, suffering and death. The only salvation lies in the extinction of this desire, and, therefore, of the kind of separate, individual human life, which generates this desire. There lies, for those who seek deliverance, a sure path to be followed, the Eightfold Path, which leads to unity and perfection. Paraphrasing the Four Noble Truths, Mr. Aldous Huxley tells us in *The Perennial Philosophy* "that the passage from the unity of spiritual to the manifoldness of temporal being is an essential part of the Fall" and "is clearly stated in the Buddhist and Hindu renderings of the Perennial Philosophy. Pain and evil are inseparable from individual existence in a world of time; and, for human beings, there is an intensification of this inevitable pain and evil when the desire is turned toward the self and the many, rather than towards the divine Ground." "We see then that, for the Perennial Philosophy, good is the separate self's conformity to and finally annihilation in the divine Ground which gives it being; evil, the intensification of separateness, the refusal to know that the Ground exists."

The Christian interpretation of suffering is not so close to this account of the perennial philosophy as Huxley assumes. The Buddhist path is one of deliverance from our unhappy human state, a state caused by what Huxley, with a Christian interpolation, calls the Fall. The Buddhist doctrine appears to go back to the very beginnings of the religion. So overcome was the Buddha at the sight of human suffering that he sought and found, as he thought, a means of deliverance from it. The kernel of the teaching is the annihilation of desire, and together with desire of the mode of existence an individual qua individual, has to live. Suffering is the chronic and incurable disease of temporal and individual life; only by abolishing the conditions of time and individuality can salvation be found. In contrast, therefore, with the Stoic view that man should reconcile himself to his place in the universe, the Buddha preached and practiced withdrawal. The Christian agrees that there is at the end of temporal life a happiness to be given to man, when "all tears will be wiped away"; he has, too, the desire to reduce all unmerited and unnecessary sufferings; but he does not regard human life as bad nor identify suffering with moral evil. The reason for this is that the world is God's creation and, therefore, good, and man no matter how disordered he may be through sin is also substantially an independent being with its own glory. He is, however, an anomaly, a bundle of contraries, a never-ending puzzle to the poet and thinker. He suffers and asks for ease from suffering, and when at ease he either falls into neglect of himself or grows so discontented that he takes on tasks which involve difficulty and pain. Suffering includes physical pain and mental distress,* and they are ambivalent. We shun suffering as a plague, but discover in time that we can extract from it, as from a poison, a remedy and a tonic.

The experience of man is reflected in the sayings and proverbs of many countries, and these pay tribute to the double effect of pain and sorrow. This effect is strikingly shown in two characteristic experiences, those of growth and love. In growth pain is so far from being an unwelcome accident that

* I exclude guilt and refer only to the effect of moral evil on others. Moral wrongdoing with its possible effect as a *felix culpa* is a separate problem.

it can be called a constituent part of it. We are accustomed to the sight of pain in the animal world and scandalized by its extreme instances, but we are more scandalized by human suffering because we assume that we should be entirely free from it. And yet a moment's thought should correct this assumption. Our case is, indeed, a complex one because the body and the mind differ in the way they develop. To the observation of Aristotle we owe this distinction. He pointed out that a spiritual act, one of the mind or will, is born complete and perfect. There are no inferior "embryonic" stages in it. In this respect it is unlike a chemical or biological process, which takes time and is incomplete until the process is ended. One thought may be connected with another, but it is always a thought and not half a one (which is different from an idea only half thought out). That is why we are, when in possession of our faculties and adults, responsible, and with a mind of our own. We say, "This is my judgment, this is my decision." We choose between possible acts and select ideas, and we are prepared to risk our reputation and destiny in a decision. At the same time we grow spiritually as well as physically. Lincoln's speeches at Springfield in 1858 and at Gettysburg in 1864 are by the same man, and both are complete, but in the intervening years Lincoln has grown in wisdom. Now the condition of a complete being, we can argue, should be one of happiness, unless it be a total failure. Happiness is felt perfection, no matter what the degree of perfection be, and so pain and sorrow have no place in such an experience. (In a material being the culmination of growth is succeeded by decay and then death or renewal of the process.) Invariably and naturally writers of stories and legends put the "heaven-haven" of the reward at the end of our mortal striving. But being, as we already are, by virtue of our spiritual principle, in a limited sense complete, we do not recognize the necessity of pain and conflict. On the contrary, we constantly delude ourselves by expecting to find in ease from pain and rest from work sheer happiness. What happens instead is that life becomes tedious, and our physical and spiritual muscles degenerate.

This truth has been forcefully set forth by Mr. Scott Edward. "Where there is no resistance," he writes, "energy can have no power. Eagles' wings beat in vain within a vacuum. Strength of mind and character, like strength of heart and limb, develop only from continuous and steadily increasing effort. Remove resistances or let determination die and very soon degeneration must set in. The mind turns slowly to fatuity; the muscles run rapidly to fat." He then illustrates his point from the history of the living cell, and the fact that many prevalent diseases of today are due to premature degeneration from lack of use. What Mr. Scott Edward says of the cell is true equally of the human organism as a whole and of human temporal growth; and the gist of it all is that growth of its very nature entails effort, suffering, loss and gain. Heraclitus in his images of the taut bow and of fire hit on this characteristic of natural processes and human experience. Pain is not just the shadow darkening human joys; joys are intermingled with pain and can be enhanced by it. Neither pain nor grief is necessarily a destroyer. We cannot climb without effort nor hold to what is honorable or lovely without pain, and the more profound our attachment to friends the greater the suffering at their absence or loss.

A phrase which has become popular and has been used in grandiose contexts does belong to the process of growth. This "the dialectic of opposites" may, indeed, remain popular because it uncovers the law hidden in growth. Hegel canonized the phrase, while borrowing the notion of dialectic from the Greeks. Socrates used it as a method of eliciting the truth out of the confused arguments of those with whom he conversed. Plato extended it to mean the process whereby initial hypotheses were criticized and purified until at the end absolute, non-hypothetical truth was reached. Hegel, believing that the real was the rational and the rational the real, conceived of a dialectic which embraced all, mind and matter. Mind of its very nature proceeds from a preliminary act to its contradiction, and then reconciles the two opposites in a synthesis; and since nature is rational and God is Mind, all, be it nature, man or God, move in the dialectical rhythm of history to a supreme comprehensive unity. Marx, rejecting the logic of ideas, substituted nature for mind and presented a system in which the processes of nature move dialectically to a tool-bearing animal and thence through the same rhythm from primitive societies to the perfect society when the state withers away. In both Hegel and Marx the dialectical process is the clue to the understanding of everything. This is too much to believe; but if, more modestly, we confine the dialectic to what is imperfect and in process, it does serve to bring out what is implied in growth. What is growing has to struggle for existence, and, in the encounter with what resists it, its activities are exercised and new force generated. Until it is fully tried the powers of a being cannot be fully measured. What holds true of the mollusk and the bird of paradise is verified in human life in a still more pronounced manner. The growing pains are more severe because of the increased sensitivity and, as civilization develops, delicacy and fastidious taste increase *pari passu*. The mind adds another dimension to physical pain by its anticipation and heightened awareness of it, and moreover its fears extend beyond what is present in space and time. This anticipation is also a constant stimulus to action and to adventure. So normal is this human condition that we make obstacles and invent competitions in every walk of life, and nod our heads at the definition that genius is an infinite capacity for taking pains. We admire the pioneer and the defender of lost causes, and in legend and song it is the Spartans of Thermopylae or the Horatios at the bridge who are praised and remembered. So essential, in fact, is opposition for growth, to keep us alert and on the move that it is difficult to conceive of life without it. There has to be a bad fairy in the legend or a Mephistopheles to prove man and prick him toward his good.

Love offers us an equally good example of the intermingling of joy and suffering. The famous couplet of Catullus, "Odi et Amo," with its ending word, "excrucior," is the compendium and memorial of passionate love. Of the same order of feeling is: "The day breaks not, it is my heart." Love creates the deepest attachment possible, and therefore lays itself open to every kind of suffering, delay, disappointment, misunderstanding, separation and death. These distinctive sufferings are again part of time's dispensation; they belong to a phase of transition, to an order in which constancy is difficult and happiness is always threatened. But just because love is so precarious, so easily snatched away, so much a windfall, it has a bitter-sweet quality in the immediate experience of it, and in memory. This is what pain adds, and it is an ingredient which can belong only to a creature of growth, who knows how short lived is the flower and what a token of affection a wound may be. "There is no poppy in Castile so lovely as his open wound." If this be so, if growth involves resistances and love begets agonies, then the Buddhist is surely mistaken in wishing to deliver us from pain and effort. They are not the enemy of true life, but the fire in which the soul has to be dipped to become itself perfect.

Love is, also, associated always with sacrifice, and its strength is judged by the degree of self-giving manifested. So intimate is this connection that some regard the two as synonymous. It is the very nature of love, they say, to sacrifice all, even the self. "Many waters cannot quench love, neither can the floods drown it: if a man should give all the substance of his house for love, he shall despise it as nothing." This declaration makes no reserves, and if it were to be taken literally then self-sacrifice is of the essence of love and active in its perfect as well as in its imperfect, mortal form. We in the West who have before our minds love as between persons may be impatient at the suggestion that the language of self-sacrifice should be taken literally. "Lovers talk that way," we say; "it is appropriate, because superlatives alone will do." But the Hindu and the Buddhist tell another story. They point to human love as a hint of the truth. Earthly love is an illusion, but it points to the ideal and in the ideal no separation is possible; the self is freed of its individuality and is entirely one with the ineffable Godhead. This view is dictated by their attitude to this world. It is a world where ignorance prevails, and consequently suffering and the sense of distinct selfhood. "Yet, joy and happiness are not the normal features of the world. In fact, the opposite seems to be the rule. Why? It is because the many, the individuals move and act in complete ignorance of their true nature, their identity with the One Spirit informing and basing them, and through It with all the rest. Each looks upon himself as distinct and different from the other and his outlook is governed by this sense of separativity, the ego which gives birth to Desire to affirm himself against others, snatch enjoyment for himself at the cost of others. This effort leads to friction, conflict and suffering." *

These words of Sri Aurobindo trace suffering back not to growth but to ignorance and the bondage of desire and separate individuality. All will acknowledge that egotism separates and is an evil, and, furthermore, that there are times when the self must be mute. The scientist has to keep himself in the background; the teacher and writer have to guard against vanity, prejudice and impure vision, for "the whole atmosphere round him is full of floating suggestion; those which are his own he cannot keep pure, for he breathes a dust of decayed ideas"; and he too easily becomes a medium of the major influences of the society in which he lives. It needs an open mind as well as courage to say at times the obvious, to point out that the Emperor is wearing no clothes. The child, who has no developed individuality, is wiser than the sophisticated; he has that state of innocence or simplicity spoken of in the Gospel. In a review of an edition of William Blake's *Songs of Innocence* the writer says that such songs have to be

* *Sri and the Upanishads;* Sri Aurobindo Circle, Eleventh Number, p. 84. The words need the context for a full understanding, and to that I will refer later.

written with the *reed* of the child-god Dionysus, and *hollowed* by Prometheus who stole fire from heaven, and he adds: "the truths of the human imagination taught by the greatest of the philosophers, and given form by the most sublime of the poets, are universal, and may therefore be recognized intuitively, as Blake said, by illiterate men and little children."

In this sense of wisdom—and it is one which truly bears the marks—imagination, feeling and intellect come together in a look of wonder, and the vision, unhindered by the dust of bad habits and prejudices, is fresh and unexpected. As this kind of perception is rare and strikes the reader as original, credit is given to the person who is the author. That is to say, personality is recognized in such wisdom. But this does not settle the matter because this wisdom is only a beginning stage in the eyes of the yogi and the contemplative. What they seek is something beyond poetic vision, namely a liberation "of the individual in some transcendent Permanence that is not individualized." Wisdom in all accounts has at most analogies with poetic vision. It is a habit of mind rather than a flash of insight, and it has to be prepared for by long and at times wearisome labor. This labor is not that only of the scholar; there are also the discipline of self and the discovery of self to be made. The two are closely related. Scholarship means patient effort, attention to detail and devotion to the work which one is doing. A man of many gifts, intelligence, quickness of judgment and detection, ingenuity, brilliant guesswork, may fail because he is lazy, scamps his work, is impatient of criticism, prejudiced, self-pitying and egotistical. He is the advocate of himself and therefore anxious for his reputation, and as a consequence truth suffers. If it be not himself, it may be a party or cause, a school of thought or a religious belief. Partisanship rarely keeps company with moderation and fairness to the opponent. The opponent or rival must be shown to be wrong and stupidly or wickedly wrong. His faults, therefore, are emphasized and his virtues ignored. The rank and file of a party like hard hitting and are not satisfied by quiet debate. In some kinds of literary and spoken warfare a convention and tradition appear to permit exaggeration and even any form of expression which is not libelous. There may be some excuse for this in political and social party warfare; but it should have no place in the quiet groves of scientific and philosophic debate or on the high places of religion. Some religions are hostile to reason and it is no wonder, therefore, if, when such strong passions are engaged, fair comment is replaced by bigotry. Since, however, truth is sacred it is lamentable when misunderstandings of another point of view in religion are due to indifference or dislike; and it is not only the devotees of a non-rational religious experience who sin in this matter. To embrace a truth and to enjoy defending it are almost part of the same experience, and it is easy to pass into a state of mind in which those who do not agree are enemies and those who are critics must be possessed of an evil will. Christians have a special temptation in that they are so sure of their own position and of its plain truth. They can assume as a result that the arguments of their adversaries must not only be wrong, but manifestly wrong, and from this assumption it is only one step to be careless about the validity of the particular argument they are called upon to use and not to bother to understand the force of the argument brought against them. They lean against the tree of life, thinking its strength to be their own personal accomplishment, and eye those who wander afield as a lost tribe of Israel, perverse and depraved. They do not realize that they have become exhibitionists and not witnesses to the truth. This vulgarization of a noble cause affects so many. It is seen in the racial conflicts, in the superior race mentality, and it manifests itself alike in the Communist propaganda against Western society and in the bourgeois reluctance to ask how and why the Marxist philosophy has captivated so many minds.

We bring ourselves into all our judgments, and if there be a lie in the soul, a beam in the eye, reality takes on a look of ourselves. It becomes not God's creation, but man's artifice. As we have seen, even the scholar is under vow to be patient and so wedded to exactness that he be not turned aside by criticism and dislike of the work of rivals. He has to drag himself to look up a reference, to wait for further evidence, and not go beyond it. In historical writing and in literary criticism there is more room for private judgment than in the specialized work in a laboratory. Every scholar can be wise within degrees, but wisdom belongs more appropriately to one who has for aim to find ultimate meanings in the nature of man and in the universe he confronts. He has to mate fact with value. The tendency in modern philosophy and even in such studies as history and literature and art is to eliminate value as adding nothing to the subject matter and therefore as irrelevant. But the philosopher who ignores values turns his back on life—the very life he should examine. He is like the man who loved colors—not flowers. "Their motion, not the swallows' wings and wasted more than half his hours without the comradeship of things." Nothing that is human is alien from a genuine philosophy, and if morals and religion cannot be reduced to the language of propositions favored by the modern analyst, so much the worse for that language. Dr. Paul Tillich has somewhat dubiously identified religion with the feeling of "ultimate concern." To make sense of the workings of nature and the history of man may be called also the task of philosophy and a matter of ultimate concern to every single man. Those who have spoken most convincingly on this subject are thought of as the wise par excellence. It is clear, however, that the shallow and the vain, the narrow-minded and the misanthropic are incapable of such wisdom; they bring themselves into their judgments, and their judgments are saturated with their weaknesses. This is the reason why in the East there still persists the belief that the sage or wise man needs a long purification of his feelings and desires as well as of his thought. Otherwise, to quote a remark of Wyndham Lewis, from his head "no thought can come before it has slipped on its uniform." Christianity is equally emphatic on the need for self-discipline and self-detachment, though its aim may be said to be different from that of the Eastern religions. All Christian asceticism and self-denial are commanded by man's supernatural calling to share in the life of God, to be "as a spouse adorned for her husband"; but what is supernatural has its echo in the universal aspiration to pass into a form of living higher than that experienced in the present. Everyday experience shows that dissatisfaction, and, what is still more embarrassing, it exhibits an alienation or split within the self. We are of a mongrel breed, half angel and half beast. Our kinship with the animals is obvious, and the evidence for our spiritual genealogy abounds in the records of literature and religion.

Some form of idealistic philosophy is as recurrent as the spring, testifying in an exaggerated form to man's belief in his spiritual nature and destiny. The kind of ideas, too, which are grouped together under the name of Gnosticism mirrors in a distorted way some fundamental human craving. The new discoveries in 1946 of some Gnostic writings show that scholars who have linked together a number of heresies down the ages were right. There is a strange disposition to believe that the soul is an element of the divine, broken off or straying in this material world which it despises. In the East so strong has this feeling been that the chief religions harp on one note, the misery and untruth of accepting this world as substantial or final. If we were to count heads, there is little doubt that a larger proportion of the human race has denied the values of this world instead of accepting them. To the man in the street of Chicago or Manchester and to the students of our technical institutes such a statement will no doubt be so incredible as to stir mirth rather than reflection.

St. Paul wrote of the spiritual and carnal man, and some such division runs through literature, whether the division be moral or religious or philosophical. There are bodily lust and spiritual love, body and mind, and the distinction between our phenomenal and real selves. The division, if accepted, may help to explain why we are interiorly so at loggerheads and "off the beam" in regard to appearance, dispositions and purposes. "Nature in all her parcels and faculties" gapes and falls apart. Like the characters in *The Confidential Clerk,* we are all confused about our real parentage and identity. The task of discovering ourselves and where we want to go is a lifelong occupation, though it be interrupted at times by a flash of illumination in the presence of love and truth and in moments of crisis. The sages smile when we talk glibly of being single-minded and honest with ourselves. There is too much veneer superimposed on the portrait to make judgment easy. The Zen Japanese artists tell us that the potter does not so much create the god as discover it in the clay, as if the god were clamoring to come out and were doing all the work. We are our own raw material, and the true self is clamoring to be seen. "We should not be searching for him had we not in a sense already found him." But there is the rub. What self? Which I? "Me? or me that fought him?"

The individual as studied by the psychologist and sociologist is a complex of many influences, and what can be computed from without corresponds in part with what is known from within. He is fashioned by heredity and environment, by family and school and by his companions and early impressions. But the individual from within has that singular and individual taste of himself which no one else can share, and he knows too that he himself is the driving force which is responsible for what he has come to be. One of the fundamental laws of his growth is by assimilation, by conscious and unconscious conformity of himself with what he likes. What we love we become, and it is this law which can confine or enlarge the dimensions of the person and at the same time make the world he has adopted his world and the only one worth saving and living in. Desires for something else or for something better may prick the conscience, though at diminishing intervals—but in becoming what he likes the individual drains off the other desires except in so far as they can feed the self which is his choice. This it is which makes the businessman contemptuous of the other-worldly, the tough despise the poet, the selfish be indifferent to the fate of those around him. The point is that these types come to believe that what they are is both normal and right; they are sure of themselves and of their standards and values. The self fastens its individuality round such an attitude, thereby making sure that it will be recognized as distinct from the herd. There is something to hold on to in a kaleidoscopic world, a mode of self-assertion, which helps to explain why the least informed are as free of their opinions on vast questions, political, national, international and even scientific, as the expert. They take up an attitude which saves their face and expresses the half-conscious belief in the rights and grandeur of every person. The trouble is that having taken to their hearts a most inadequate idea of the universe and life, and at the same time having drunk in without reflection the contemporary ideas of the market place, they are far from having that simplicity of vision and unprejudiced self which lead on to wisdom.

That no one is so buried under false beliefs and so evilly disposed that he cannot be made to see truth is the optimistic belief of Christianity. Some religions would separate here and now the sheep from the goats, the free from the naturally slavish. There is said to be an inflexible law of karma, and inferior lives must be repeated in a transmigration to other forms. Only the chosen souls can be emancipated and become one with the divine. It is here that those who favor a perennial philosophy shared by all mystics and high philosophers part company from the Christian. The Christian would have all enter into a bliss offered by a living God and will not allow that personality need ever be diminished. When the divine love intervenes the darkness of sight of even those most shut in can be dispersed. True knowledge, contemplation and wisdom are made possible when we love God—for we become what we love. But, say the other side, we become indeed what we love, and there is no longer place for the I, for that self which has been all the time the obstacle in the way. The late Ananda K. Coomaraswamy believed that Christianity in its essence taught no other doctrine than that of Hinduism. He tells us in a paper on *The Indian Doctrine of Man's Last End* that "in Indian scriptures the qualifications of one who is enabled to pass through the Sun and enter into the Godhead 'as milk might be poured into milk' are primarily those of Truth and Anonymity. . . . One who reaches the end of the road and enters into God must leave behind him the whole burden of his deeds, whether good or evil. For these are the basis of 'character,' and nothing characteristic can enter into the uncharacterized Deity, 'Whose only idiosyncrasy is being.' " He then quotes Meister Eckhart to support these statements and continues: "The consciousness of a man can be centred in his body, and this is the animal man; or in the soul, and this is the psychic man; or in the spirit, which is the spiritual or pneumatic man. It is the latter alone that can 'return' to God in likeness of nature. Nor is this last end of man merely a matter of *post mortem* destiny; for 'the kingdom of heaven is within you,' or as the Upanishad expresses it, 'The inconceivable form of Deity, farther than far away, and also here within you, though It cannot be seen by the eye's intrinsic faculty, can be appreciated by Truth, and can be seen by the illuminated Gnostic, where It indwells the secret chamber of the heart. . . .' The Hindu 'deification,' then, is precisely what is meant when we are commanded 'Be ye therefore perfect, even as your Father in Heaven is perfect,' and meant by St. Paul when he says that 'Whoever is joined unto the Lord is one Spirit.' . . ."

This interpretation of Coomaraswamy's will not, I fear, be acceptable to Christians or Hindus. In his recent translation and edition of *The Principal Upanishads* Dr. S. Radhakrishnan assumes as certain the identity of the individual self with the universal Atman and tells us that "while the poets of the Veda speak to us of the many into which the radiance of the Supreme has split, the philosophers of the Upanishads speak to us of the One Reality behind and beyond the flux of the world." It seems to me unhistorical to suppose that the Jewish writers of the New Testament, with their belief in one living God, could have had in mind the idea of deity and of the self portrayed by Coomaraswamy. Eckhart, whom he quotes in evidence, is not a safe guide in Christian theology or mysticism and has never been ranked with Ruysbroeck, St. Teresa or St. John of the Cross. The first great mystery of the Christian Revelation stands blocking the way followed by Indian monists, that essential doctrine that in one God there are three Persons. Without persons and personality there is no Christian religion, and its philosophy centers round this thought that, whereas in brute matter anonymity reigns rather than individuality, as we ascend the scale separate individualities begin to emerge until in man selfhood is found, the image of that life where the richest personality abounds.

Although, as we have seen it personal experience with its liberty and independence is the special grace of human life, nevertheless it must be owned that there are difficulties in the conception, difficulties, philosophic and religious, which no doubt lie behind the Oriental disparagement of it. The philosophic difficulty is this: our individuality is dependent on what is odd and unimportant and has no place in the higher regions of thought. If we ask how one man differs from another we have to point to variations in shape and in body, in nerves and glands, in feeling and emotional reactions, in heritage and environment. These variations are all accidental and can be described as idiosyncrasies, which, like fashions, break the monotony and routine of nature. Life would be intolerable without them, but they belong to the evanescent world of the senses, and they impede intellectual pursuits. Reason seeks to unite the disparate, to discover uniformities and law. The coelacanth is interesting as a specimen of a supposedly defunct species, not because of its individual attractiveness. The scientist is engaged on something common to himself and his fellow workers. He knows that he has a personal equation and he tries to reduce its interference to a minimum; he has to work with a clockwork precision, and he regards it as an obstacle that he cannot in his observations and experiments avoid all relativity and do what the child said of God, that He made a stool to sit on and then created the world. What is true of the scientist holds also for the logician and metaphysician. The metaphysician strives to see reality as it is, and if he and his compeers did attain to truth, then they would all be looking at the same identical truth and having an identical experience. In such a condition all that is individual and erratic would have been swept away and minds would meet and merge in one thought.

So deep-set is the unity of soul and body that the spheres of influence of each remain always corrigible. Physiology pushes forward its frontiers on one side, psychoanalysis on the other, but the unity remains such as to give the lie to the argument just stated. What have been called the accidental variations due to the body and to time and place are a material which is formed by some inner agency and in the forming made human and personal. The professional philosophers, as Mr. G. H. Spinney, in an article in *Philosophy* has pointed out, tend to neglect what he calls "will" in their explanation of perception and knowledge. Throughout our experience, so he contends, there is this activity of "will," which brings order into the series of sense data. "When we strive to push a car up a slope and fail and it runs back on us, we are not merely the surprised observers of a sensory experience that has gone contrary to our expectations, but we experience a frustration of nascent subjective order, as though the cogs were slipping within our will. There is this important difference, that the connectedness of the will at the level of intuition is self-guaranteed, while that which counters our will has only a phenomenal connectedness. We have no insight into it. For example, when A and B engage in a tug of war, while A is aware at each moment of opposition to his will, the assumption that it is due to the counter-will of B, having a progressively deployed internal connectedness like his own, is an inference based on analogy, not a fact of direct observation." He goes on to show that our recognition of other minds arises from the analogy with our own conscious experience of personal activity. Now it is this ultimate subject of all we think, construct and do which gives the uniqueness and incommunicable character to the self. For a picture of what this ultimate subject can be we can draw on the poet, Gerard Hopkins and his idea of "inscape" and "instress." We have to suppose a bare self, which is a positive infinitesimal and intrinsically different from every other self. This self is like the nod of the head which says yes or no at every step of its growth or progress. It is clothed with a nature, human nature, and this gives it a field of operation and room for choice. Given this distinctness and freedom, the self takes on more and more a separate and marked character. It is partly determined and partly self-determining, but even where it has to accept consciously or unconsciously the myriad influences of the external world or impose its own will upon them, it is all the time adapting what it receives to its own pitch of being, and what it is, and what it is becoming, are visible in all that it does. We can distinguish an inner and outer side, the self and the expression of the self. As in a house long lived in, everything tells us in its own way of its owner's personality, the decoration of the rooms and the books upon the shelves, so, as Hopkins says, the self "deals out that being indoors (where) each one dwells." This it is which makes the style of a writer, the score of a musician, so unmistakable; there is present the personal accent or inflection, the signature tune.

Such a description of selfhood enables us to see that the unity of mind and matter in each individual cannot be so separated as to apportion individuality to material accidents of time and place. This is obvious if we take examples from those who by general consent are pre-eminent in history among the company they keep, Dante, Michelangelo, Bach or Spinoza. No matter how abstract the thought of Spinoza we are made conscious of his high-minded and unworldly character in the writing. Again no one could mistake the best Shakespearean plays for those by any other dramatist, and what he writes is all compact of thought and imagination and sensibility; it is a human individuality, and not one made up of bodily identifying marks. We do not need his fingerprints. There are, it is true, copies of masterpieces so skillfully done that even the elect are for a while deceived. But, to take the instance of painting, the imitation is usually of only one picture. Close copies, indeed, confirm my argument, for if at first we are deceived, further acquaintance makes us aware of something lacking. What this lack is may be hard to explain to another, and we are forced back onto saying that the copy is dead; the vibrant and incommunicable originality of the author is missing.

If then there be this never-to-be-repeated selfhood, which cannot be reduced to physical variations, has it any properties by which we can recognize it? I suggest that there are at least three. The first of these is originality or what is often called creative power. In the works of genius this is very pronounced, but it is the possession of everyone. It follows from the freedom of every individual and from his choosing to be instead of not to be. The unique self develops that originality in its multiple choices as it grows, blurring no doubt that work of art which is itself by wrong choices and surrenders, and distinguishing it with good choices. The counting of heads, the numbering of men and women for a race or for a census are justified because of their convenience for the purpose in hand. The employees in a factory are leveled down to a multitude by the common function they are performing, but as representatives of human nature and its embodiments each is a complete human being and like no other; and this is one of the reasons why the problem of a state consists in having to combine both the general interests and the interests and independent responsibilities of each of the citizens. The evil again of a Communist society lies in treating all citizens as identical and trying to reduce them to a condition in which their behavior is communal and not personal. The second property lies in the power of communication. Human beings, so far as we know, alone have developed a language. They have ideas of themselves and of others; they are so self-conscious that they can express themselves to themselves and to others, and this expression has been called the persona or mask, the personification. This self-expression plays an important part in the development of self, for one sees one's self in part and can examine it and realize its uniqueness and loneliness. It serves as well as a kind of Indian's rope on which to climb. By means of an ideal of one's own devising all the activities of the self, conscious and subconscious, are brought into co-operation, and the self grows into what it is bent on becoming. Communication is not however merely with oneself; there is the logos in its two aspects of idea and of speech symbol. As idea the self can remake in its own terms what lies outside itself, learning something of the nature of every conceivable thing, its logos or definition, and so it possesses its own private version of the cosmos. By speech we enter into communication with other persons. Unique as personality is, it is not sufficient for itself. The idiot is the person deprived of communication, and it is by the give and take of signs and speech that the growth of each single person is insured. Lastly there is love. It is by love that we come to appreciate the unique quality of every individual. The lover

discovers that there is nobody else in the world like the beloved
and in being herself she is incomparable and inexhaustible.
There is no monotony in love and no anonymity; it leads to
the closest of all unions by emphasizing the distinctiveness of
persons.

> So when from hence we shall be gone,
> And be no more, nor you, nor I,
> As one another's mystery,
> Each shall be both, yet both but one.

Originality and loneliness, self-consciousness and communication, communication and love, these three, coming together
like the lines of a triangle, compose what we mean by personality. A finite personality no doubt, but in its triunity showing a far-off resemblance to what is revealed in the Christian
mystery of divine perfection, of God who is three persons in
one nature, a Father and source, a Logos or word, and a spirit
of Charity.

If this be true, then the craving to lose oneself, the desire of
the Absolute, which undoes the finite, the dissatisfaction with
the individual, can be temptations which, if yielded to, will
bring at most half answers, and at the worst, disintegration.
The individual as we know him is certainly not self-sufficient.
His character can be changed, and is at times unrecognizable
even to himself. He is in so many respects a part or member
of some group or society larger than himself, and he vanishes
to a point of reference in the large-scale maps of the universe.
Philosophy, as the existentialists have complained, omits the
plight of the individual. It is concerned with natures, with
categories, with the universal, and moves, if not watched, into

the realms of the necessary, when "things are what they are, and their consequences will be what they will be; (so) why then should we seek to be deceived?" And if the mystic starts with his own private concern, with things as they appear to him, he is made so conscious of the ebb and flow of the temporal and the tantalizing half lights of present experience that he is moved to indict it all and sacrifice everything, our finite personality included, for the sake of a transpersonal and subsistent reality. The individual, indeed, is beset on all sides, and has to look far and wide for protection. To the empiricist he is a complicated product of nature; to the psychologist a character, which can be resolved into its components and reconditioned. Personality has become just another word for character, and so the true meaning of "person" has gone with the wind. Those who employ the word and provide techniques for higher knowledge have borrowed from the vocabulary and techniques of the Eastern mystics. They tell us that there are layers of so-called selfhood which have to be stripped away, until the true being of the initiate is exposed, his identity, that is, with the source or plenitude of being.

The process and the experience of finding one's true self have been so often described, and in such similar language, that something corresponding to the stripping off of layers must be admitted even by the skeptical. Nevertheless the experience is so private and so intense and so hard to measure that there is plenty of room for error. I have already referred to the centrifugal movement of the self, which is present in some of the ecstatic religions and makes itself felt in the swoon of self-surrender. This movement may enter into an exalted mystic condition, and so give the illusion that the self is absorbed in some ultimate being or reality. We have to remember that all our inner experiences are difficult to interpret and to express, and the difficulty starts with the mysterious power of being self-conscious. If the self we are conscious of within were our total self, all might be simple. But the self we see is, as it were, in a mirror, which can be flattering or deceptive, so that, while others can never know us as we know ourselves, they can at times have a more dispassionate and accurate idea of our motives and character. Many hate the sight of themselves and dare not face it, and they play with a substitute until it becomes a second nature. The politician, the successful businessman, the university professor often look into distorting mirrors, and most young people live in a state of uncertainty of what they are like. As many cases have proved, men and women can become so chameleonlike that the parts they play separate into split personalities. That this does not affect the one subsistent person as such is proved by its capacity to reunite once more the split parts. True self-knowledge, therefore, is an ideal, and always demanding patience and discipline and meditation, as well as honesty. The philosophers tell us, and in this they are borne out by everyday experience, that we have no direct acquaintance or intuition of our substantial self. This means that we cannot be directly aware of the subject which grows. Moreover, as we are in process of growth all the length of our days, there is no prospect of our reaching that ideal knowledge of the finished product.

The techniques of the Eastern sages are directed to taking us out of the shadows and the world of phantasmagoria into the pure light of truth. The Christian contemplatives also insist on a path or ladder of perfection. The ephemeral, the worldly, has to be denied, the self-bound concepts and desires forsaken, and then out of the night the soul may pass to a new understanding and experience. The Christian contemplative, however, claims that the self is thereby made more perfect and does not lose its identity. Most of the texts of the Hindu and Buddhist literature, on the other hand, appear to require the disappearance of the self. According to some this is due to the fact that all the language of self and all our human concepts break down utterly when confronted with the ineffable mystery of union. Others can find no place for any individuality in that perfection of being which alone is real. To mitigate this some confine the meaning of self to that egotistic being which fights for itself and would live in the world of separateness and pain. The differences are such that an Eastern sage can still seek to clarify some of the philosophy and reinterpret the Veda and the Upanishads. This is what has been done by the late Sri Aurobindo, scholar and mystic. Of Buddhism, for instance, he writes: "Buddhism is of many kinds and the entirely nihilistic kind is only one variety"; and in another letter: "In the Buddhistic Nirvana they feel as if there were no such thing at all (as existence), only an infinite zero without form. In the Adwaita Nirvana there is felt only one Vast Existence, no separate being is discernible anywhere. . . . Sometimes there is only the consciousness of pure existence, sometimes only pure consciousness, sometimes all that exists is only a ceaseless limitless Ananda. Whether all else is really dissolved or only covered up is a debatable point, but at any rate it is an experience as if of their dissolution."

He himself is so chaste of mind, so experienced, and so wide in his philosophical sympathy that he can be accepted as a

Hindu model of an unprejudiced perennial philosophy. Writing, for instance, of man's "supreme goal" he says: "So dazzling is even a glimpse of this supreme existence and so absorbing its attraction that, once seen, we feel readily justified in neglecting all else for its pursuit. Even by an opposite exaggeration to that which sees all things in Mind and the mental life as an exclusive ideal, Mind comes to be regarded as an unworthy deformation and a supreme obstacle, the source of an illusory universe, a negation of the Truth and itself to be denied and all its works and results annulled if we desire the final liberation. But this is a half truth which errs by regarding only the actual limitations of Mind and ignores its divine intention. The ultimate knowledge is that which perceives and accepts God in the universe as well as beyond the universe and the integral Yoga is that which, having found the Transcendent, can return upon the universe and possess it, retaining the power freely to descend as well as ascend the great stair of existence. For if the eternal Wisdom exist at all, the faculty of Mind also must have some high use and destiny. That use must depend upon its place in the ascent and in the return and that destiny must be a fulfilment and transfiguration, not a rooting out or an annulment." Every reader will notice in this passage the generosity of Sri Aurobindo's thought and how it eschews the negation or annulment of human life. It is not a nirvana as usually understood, nor is the state of perfection so out of touch with this world as to take all meaning from human life. The wise man has his work to do here on earth, and the language in which this part is couched changes from the impersonal deity to a living God. The movement of ascent and return has echoes in it of the going forth of creatures and their return in St. Thomas Aquinas, and, be it said, also of the from-and-to process in Plotinus and Hegel. But these very resemblances and the ecumenical language he uses raise a doubt and remind one of what he says in criticism of the Mahayana Buddhism, that it "tries to give an added and superlative force and value to its ideas and tenets, but only succeeds in making them vulnerable." A description is weak when its language can mean more than one thing, things, that is, which have different associations and may be incompatible. God cannot be both transcendent and with a "divine intention" and be at the same time all reality. If he is, then either all reality, no matter what its imperfections, is divine, or all that is imperfect must turn out to be unreal. The evolutionary process, which is introduced, only complicates the problem. The Isha Upanishad, we are told, teaches that "the universe is a movement of the Spirit. It is a continuous unrolling of the Spirit in myriad forms which are so many currents of the Great Movement. Each form is a front, a shaping of the general stream in an individualised unit. Each one has the Whole behind, sustaining it, and thus constitutes a universe in itself." The purpose of the movement "is to provide a habitation for God for his enjoyment. The individual is a living term and front of this manifestation and should share in this enjoyment; but his ignorance of his true nature shuts him from this happiness and gives rise to the ego-sense of a separate self-giving and its consequent struggle and strife."

There is again in this passage so much that can be welcomed: the intention of God, the calling by God of the individual to share his enjoyment and the obstacle of self-will. In such language, though it may seem to smack too much of the unfashionable Hegelian idealism to please English-speaking philosophers, there is a bridge between East and West. The lair of nirvana, from which there are no human footsteps returning, is replaced by a Spirit, whose habitation is happiness, and who gives happiness to human individuals and a purpose in this life. Such teaching corrects the prevalent empirical outlook of the West, and reminds it of a wisdom with which it was once more familiar. It does not, however, speak in such clear-cut terms that the ambiguities, already mentioned, are removed. The relations between the Spirit and the "myriad forms," our human selves, remain obscure. The self seems to belong in some way to the Spirit by right, as if possessing the same nature, and only prevented from union with it by ignorance. The self, again, in so far as it is self-seeking and separatist is a false unit and must die; and this is the common teaching of all the spiritual philosophies. But it is not clear what self remains at the end, nor how there could be one at all, if only ignorance separates it from the Most High, and not personal choices, good and bad, proceeding from its finite nature. Nor can this obscurity be attributed to beggarly words, to our inability to speak or breathe on these Pisgah heights. The partial successes of the saints and seers and philosophers in distinguishing what can be said and what cannot be said are proof that there is a right and wrong use of language, and that thought does not entirely founder. If thought did founder the great literature of Buddhism and Hinduism would founder with it.

The Christian philosophy transposes the language used above into that of persons. God is a living spirit and can in no sense be identified with the world or any process of it, however close to it his creative and sustaining activity may be. Man too is a finite, personal being, who could never possibly by any effort of his own attain to divinity. Man is not only ignorant; he can never know perfectly, and that is why the more he meditates and by self-denial understands himself, the more humble does he become. It is this virtue of humility which is the clue to true wisdom; and it is this same virtue which brings to light the kind of permanent being which every individual man has. Hindu, Buddhist and Christian are at one in their insistence on prayer, self-knowledge and self-denial. In this school of perfection the senses, passions and desires have to be purified and disciplined into order, the will rectified and the mind enlightened, and by these means and others, according to Christian teaching, egotism decreases, but the self does not fade out; it grows more humble. Such a philosophy of the self does not depart from common opinion. We take for granted that we are the same person through the years; any mother and father would be bewildered if they were told that the son they see now is as distinct from the child they reared as the Tichborne claimant from the original heir. What is paradoxical is that we aspire to be ourselves more and more, to make something of our talents and character and intelligence, and so be ourselves; and at the same time there is a movement in us to lose ourselves in something greater, to become what we love. This is the mysterious dual activity of the self; its action and passion, its inhalation and exhalation. The self must grow and be complete, and it cannot do so without becoming so interested in objects or persons as to forget and even sacrifice its own interests. Self-interest, therefore, and constant introspection, if pursued by themselves, produce a hypertrophied self. It feeds on distorted images, which need to be corrected by a dose of the real. To set the balance right the mind and will must not only abide by the evidence of facts; they need also some objective ideal, which demands self-sacrifice. Then the self, which is the object of consciousness, comes nearer to the subject who is thinking and willing, as we see actually happening when a man is taken up with a cause or a lover with his beloved. So close can this approximation come that the mind seems to be absent from itself and be no longer observant of its own states and interests. This condition it is, no doubt, which leads so many of the high-minded to believe that the self will finally be absorbed in a loftier and more comprehensive reality. Much, let it be admitted, does depend upon the object of the love. There are objects or beings which are said to steal the heart away, Circes which mesmerize their victims and leave them semi-human. They cannot altogether destroy, but they can reduce the exercise of freedom and personality to a minimum. Such nether gods are, however, put to flight by the true God and by true love. Ideals and persons do not enthrall and take away; they give integrity and magnify the powers of the mind and will, the while they inhibit calculation, self-interest and second thoughts. An image, faulty but suggestive, of the interplay of self-regard and selflessness is provided by the actor on the stage. He is said so to identify himself with the part he is playing that he becomes the character and makes the audience forget the man behind the part. Now such an actor will speak of the concentration needed and of the upset caused by any interruption or distraction; yet he will also maintain that he is more himself and aloofly aware of the part he is playing, the while he appears to be and is lost in it. The self depicted here is the mainspring and conscious determinant of all the actor does, and the more concentrated it is the nearer does it come to its proper and perfect activity. The nature and process of growth entail this kind of dichotomy within ourselves; we who are free determinants of what we shall be have to look at and superintend the growth; and the watcher and the observed come together when we are fully occupied, a foretaste of a perfect state when we shall no longer be strangers to ourselves. Loss of that self-consciousness which divides us does not spell disintegration but a degree of completeness. If we knew ourselves wholly, the object-self and the subject-self would no longer be distinct; we should be fully active, and in that activity our mind and will would be cleaving to what gives us incomparable and unending happiness. That object, in the Christian philosophy, is the living God, and it is his compresence which makes us realize in him what we are. In the knowing of God and in the loving of him we shall see ourselves without the need of an extra act of self-awareness. It is as if a score of music could be conscious and burst into sound; and in that very act it would be conscious of its theme and make-up by knowing and loving the creator of itself. The created act and the creative act come together. The human finite person remains at one with himself and at one with divine love. In that reciprocal love we cannot talk of an identity without difference. For that union difference is essential, the difference which always exists in a personal relationship of giving and receiving.

V.

Conclusion

MR. ALDOUS HUXLEY in entitling a book *The Perennial Philosophy* intended to give a more precise meaning to a descriptive phrase, which hitherto had served a useful if prescientific purpose. Words of wisdom handed down from the past, the proverbs and gnomic sayings of different cultures, passages from poets and seers had a family likeness; an anthology of them could be likened to the common sense of a higher order. But just as common sense is like quicksilver when we stop to catch its exact meaning, so this superior common wisdom could not be so easily determined. Catholic thinkers were for a time sure that it was to be found in the main current of Christian philosophy, and M. de Wulf attempted to say in more detail what it was. The subject once started proved more elusive than expected, and the dispute has not yet ended with general agreement. Dr. Inge, as already mentioned, and others have sought for a perennial wisdom in the happy combination of Greek and Hebrew thought with the Christian belief and inspiration. Now that the great Eastern literatures have become better known and appreciated, it was almost inevitable that a new attempt should be made to widen the meaning of

this perennial wisdom. What a contribution to human civilization if it could be shown that its wisest and best representatives
have all been in accord in their teaching on man's true way of
life and on the nature of perfection! The accord need not be
apparent at first sight. Every religion and every philosophy
bears the mark of its time; it will have its own eccentricities
and deviations, its local color and special traditions. The
Moslem and the Christian may crusade against each other, the
Hindu and Buddhist quarrel; such differences are endemic,
but superficial. They serve to disguise what is common, and
therefore the searcher must penetrate through them to discover
the highest common factor. This is what the new Gnostics
have done, and they have exhibited their discoveries.

Impressive as the similarities are, and important as bearing
on the question of human ideals and human destiny, they are
only distant likenesses, and on closer inspection decisive dis-
similarities also appear. If there be a perennial wisdom, made
up of a conflation of all high religious and philosophic thought,
it must have more modest pretensions. It bears witness to the
undying spirit of man, and it has extended beyond belief our
knowledge of his spiritual capacities. Just as modern trials and
experiments have revealed to us most unexpected powers of
the body, to live without food or amid disease, to withstand
altitudes and wind pressures, so the lives of gurus and yogis
show that the body can be so mastered by the spirit as to behave in a way outside the calculations of physical and medical
science. The inner control gained by concentration and spiritual exercises brings the senses, the actions of the heart and
brain, even dreams, into a new and preternatural collabora-
tion with the mind. The mind, in turn, or spirit enters into

experiences which, were the evidence not irrefutable, would not be believed by the hard-headed man of today. The control and bliss are such as to give a glimpse of a spiritual perfection undreamed of in our Western modern philosophies.

Mr. John Wu in his *Beyond East and West* remarks that "the average Buddhist knows something about the three stages of Abstention, of Concentration and Wisdom, whereas the average Christian has no idea of the three ways, purgative, illuminative and unitive." The sages of the East have kept alive a tradition which has grown faint in a civilization increasingly preoccupied with time and the benefits which time and technology can provide. The contemplative spirit is like an ancient title, respected perhaps, bowed to as to a relic but more an embarrassment than a privilege. The Eastern Sophia reminds us that peace comes from concentration and not dispersion of mind, and that in part "it is mind which gives things their quality, their foundation and their being. Whoever speaks or acts with impure mind, him sorrow follows, as the wheel follows the steps of the ox that draws the cart" (Dhammapada). This quest for a quiet mind is not an escape to an ivory tower, nor just a respite from action nor a luxury. Those who say or think this keep forgetting that history is against them, that from time immemorial a mode of living has been sought by high and low which would liberate the self from the slavery of the passions, the false images of time and the idols of the market place. What shows this recurrent search for spiritual peace to be grounded in human nature is the uniformity in its initial stages. The fakir or the pillar saint may appear to be a curiosity or "sport," but this cannot be said of the vast numbers who have reached a new self-control and a luminosity of spirit by adopting similar techniques of abstention and self-denial and concentration of all their powers. What is more, the ideal to which they attain does not lie off the road of human development; it spills over and, mingling with the common affairs of man, shapes it into a culture.

All the masters are agreed that wisdom surpasses knowledge, if by knowledge we mean learning and information. These latter have to be worked together into a unity, a point of view, and it is here that the self makes its contribution for good or ill. There is a relation between what we are and how we see; if the self is in love with itself or with the flesh or this world's goods, it is blind to the riches wisdom offers. The first step, therefore, is a thorough cleansing of the eye of the soul, and this requires a long discipline of the will and its desires. Capacities unused have degenerated, the mind has adapted itself to a low ceiling, and the self takes pleasure in its captivity to the passions. As Aristotle said: "When a man falls from virtue into vice, he becomes in a sense another man," and the reverse is true. When liberated and able to turn himself where he will he begins to discover his true physiognomy. For all who take up an art or a profession a degree of moral integrity is required. The artist must not fake; in his work there comes, as with the bullfighter, "the moment of truth." The scholar and the scientist have to be dispassionate in their judgments and experiments and assess the evidence fairly, recognizing the degree of probability at which they have arrived and scrapping the hypothesis if new facts tell against it. As their knowledge increases, by reason of their integrity and genius, they come to be held in high esteem and are spoken of as wise. But such wisdom, while it may be a component in a wider vision, is not what is meant by the sages and those who write about a perennial wisdom. The object of their study is too confined; it is like an aquarium compared to the ocean, or a museum compared to the mysteries of the universe and the self. The specialist and the scholar may be uninterested in what lies outside their subject, and the light of their minds goes out when they leave their manuscript or calculus behind.

They do not, therefore, belong to that company of wise men who, as it is thought, have gone behind appearances and come back with a better understanding of the meaning and order of nature and human life. Such a man would never exaggerate the relative importance of the subject matter of his study; he sees it in its proper perspective in a scale of values, which the better understanding of himself and the divine mystery gives him. His knowledge is not dependent on books; he has gathered wisdom in solitude, from friends and from nature, and through suffering. No one can escape the schooling of experience, and the spirit as well as the face bears its marks. But how we are conditioned is our own affair. We grow by what we love and fear, and the cynics and optimists have made themselves what they are. They have not wanted to know the truth about themselves, and unlike the wise they have not sought the path of purification and self-denial. The wise are those who have begun, like Socrates, with an admission of ignorance and by facing reality have dared to face truth. Psychiatrists are well aware of the need of this habit of looking at things as they are, even as a horseman forces the horse to look at the obstacle at which it panics, and the pilot, who has had a crash, hastens to fly again. But it is not ordinary facts which reveal a man to himself and teach him wisdom; he has to see himself in the at first terrifying presence of what is finally true and good, and he needs preparation to be ready for this discovery.

Until this discovery is made there is always the danger that the self, abandoning itself to self-deception, read its own false or immature values into the world around. St. Augustine tells us that after what he had learned and experienced in Carthage in his youth he took for granted that everything was material, even God. Later he changed, and the spiritual world opened for him. In Platonism, he says, he saw truth but from afar off. The Word that was with God was not yet made flesh and speaking to him personally. Wisdom came as he overcame his desires and purified his mind. The Hindu school of Sri Auro-bindo is equally insistent on the grossness of mind which comes from living too contentedly with our psycho-physical disposi-tions. "The true human existence, therefore, only begins when the intellectual mentality emerges out of the material and we begin to live more and more in the mind independent of the nervous and physical obsession" of the body. By this is meant not merely freedom from living "according to the flesh." The mind has to break free from its secondary habits, its conven-tional tastes and prejudices, which coil around it and make it captive, like Laocoon. There are moreover the forces which come from the underworld of the self and falsify reason and judgment unawares. Freedom is more than "the knowledge of necessity"; it is choice and the result of choice, an increasing power of self-determination, a leap into the fresh air, as the fish in the sea of Salamis leap above the waters to greet the rising sun. In the light of a new vision the self integrates what was disordered, and finds a connaturality with the spiritual values and beauty now for the first time clearly seen. This change is like a conversion, a cleansing and renovation for the spirit.

"Virtues," says Thomassin, "are not conditions of the soul resting in itself, but leaps of the soul away from itself into God." This is the common teaching of all the religious philosophies of East and West, and it makes a good beginning. But thence onward the ways begin to separate. What place have the world of appearances and the self as the search goes on and wisdom declares itself? Buddha, so far as can be known, taught the way of release from misery; that way was through the extinction of desire. Individuality is the breeding ground of desires, and therefore by the emancipation from it, and by the overcoming of the duality caused by ignorance, we arrive at Nirvana. Of Nirvana Buddha did not try to give an explanation. As in all great systems, however, different interpretations have been given. It is the "nothing which is all"; it is the permanent beyond the realm of Karma and Sankaras; it is an ineffable state beyond and above all concepts. In all the interpretations this world and the self are finally of no account. To the Platonists this world is half unreal, a world of phenomena, which corresponds with our ordinary human outlook, darkened as that is because of our dependence on the senses. Amongst the great Hindu thinkers there are some who take a view of human life similar to that of the Buddhists. The Buddhist system, indeed, is merely one conspicuous example of the tendency in Eastern philosophy to make nought of what is finite and subject to change and death. Its eyes are on the infinite, and its bane is duality and separation wherever encountered. So rich, however, is the literature on which Hindu thinkers can rely that the philosophy of the problem of the One

and the Many has flowered into many varieties. This problem
has its twin in the nature of the state of Bliss. The solution,
already mentioned of Sri Aurobindo, based on an intimate
knowledge of the Hindu scriptures, tries to meet modern science
on its own ground and is inspired by personal spiritual experience. In his view nature and human development are not
without worth. He accepts a kind of cosmic evolution, Spirit
making a progressive self-manifestation in nature and man. He
does not, therefore, stop at a negative, at the renunciation of
all desire. "It can be, therefore, no integral Yoga which ignores
the body or makes its annulment or its rejection indispensable
to a perfect spirituality. Rather, the perfecting of the body also
should be the last triumph of the Spirit. . . ." Asceticism is
required to free the mind from the thralldom of the senses.
Man has to reach a full intellectual life. But this is not the
end; he has to evolve into something higher. "The assertion
of a higher than the mental life is the whole foundation of
Indian philosophy and its acquisition and organisation is the
veritable object served by the methods of Yoga." This higher
state is a "pure self-existent and self-luminous Truth. And this
bliss is not a supreme pleasure of the heart and sensations with
the experience of pain and sorrow in the background, but a
delight also self-existent and independent of objects and particular experiences, a self-delight which is the very nature, the
very stuff, as it were, of a transcendent and infinite existence."
In a letter he repeats that "the Indian view is that the Divine is
the inmost substance of the universe, but he is also outside it,
transcendent; good and evil, happiness and misery are only
phenomena of cosmic experience due to a division and a dimi-
nution of consciousness in the manifestation but are not part

of the essence or of the undivided whole-consciousness either of the Divine or of our own spiritual being." Now our spiritual gnosis, as he calls it, consists in lifting the soul up into this supermental state, which is one of bliss and union with the divine spirit. The process needs the most careful direction, lest the novice overreach himself and try to be what he is still ill prepared for. The mind still dependent on its mental forms has to convert them into that spiritual gnosis which is one with divinity itself. This is possible because "there is a transcendent existence, supreme self or spirit, a timeless soul of existence, an eternal, a Divine, or even we may speak of it in relation to current mental ideas of the Godhead as a supra-Divine, which is here immanent, all embracing, all initiating and all governing, a great universal Spirit; and the individual is a conscious power of being of the Eternal, capable of relations with him, but one with him too in the very core of reality of its own existence."

There are echoes of many philosophies in these passages, and the word *gnosis* suggests a higher and inner knowledge shared by all those who have reached that "higher state beyond the mental life," which is wisdom. This is, therefore, a more specified form of what is called perennial wisdom by Mr. Aldous Huxley. It gathers together the pieces—nature, self, this human world of striving and pain, thought and a state of bliss beyond thought, the transcendence and immanence of the divine Spirit—and tries to fit them together, each in its proper place, in a religious cosmos. It is not new. The same syncretic tendency showed itself in the early centuries of Christianity, and some of the terms used then reappear in the modern gnosis. Man has a body, a psyche and a nous, and corresponding with these are regions of reality one above the other: the sublunary earth, the sphere of the Sun and Moon and the fixed stars and highest of all the third heaven, where was to be found a superessential reality, where God dwells. The Christian writers were not afraid to use this imagery, common to the Eastern and Neo-Platonic thought; St. Paul speaks of being rapt into the third heaven, St. Justin of the "supercelestial place" where God has his habitation, and as is well known Denys the Areopagite provided a kind of textbook for Christian contemplatives. The story, even, of Buddha's conversion has found its way into the early Christian lives of Sts. Barlaam and Josaphat. But this good will shown by the early Christian thinkers toward current ideas, and adaptation of their language, did not signify any compromise. Syncretism was the aim of the Gnostics, and the Christians regarded such syncretism as a wishful dream or specious forgery of its own wisdom. It presented man with a picture of himself as so like to God as to be of his nature. Man the image was transformed into the original, and all that belonged to him as merely human was perishable and of no account. The abyss between the finite and the infinite disappeared.

This Gnostic sophia has an undying attraction. It offers emancipation to men and women from all the agonies of human living; it frees them from the formulas and imperfections of creeds, from attachment to self, to time and place and body. It etherealizes all, till in the end thought and desire lose their sting and all is to be well in the calm and plenitude of an ineffable bliss. In a civilization so attached to liberty and individualism as the West such an ideal, it might be thought, could never be popular. It has not, it is true, had the same success in the West as in the East; but this may well be due to the permeation by the Christian philosophy. Even within that philosophy there have been occasional epidemics, such as the doctrine of predestination and Neo-Platonic idealism. The former gained a strong hold in Calvinism, and geniuses, like Scotus Eriugena and Eckhart were tinged with the latter. What is more remarkable is its reappearance in the seventeenth century in the center of Catholic culture under the form of quietism. The name is new, but the doctrine is fundamentally gnostic. Molinos, its chief exponent, and Madame Guyon taught that the soul is original, pure and of divine origin, that it can return to the divine essence only by the denial of the material world of sense and marriage. The soul must annihilate itself in its active being, and be transformed back into its pure state of identity with God.

This claim to be part of divinity, so startling to the ordinary man, is not to be attributed to an insane pride. Pride may enter in as in the story of man's first temptation; "ye shall be gods." The ground for the claim must be sought in human nature. There is at first a craving, which can become ungovernable, for self-giving—what the word *ecstasy* literally means—to be outside and beyond oneself, and it shows itself in the flight of the self from shadows to reality, from the finite to the source of being. This craving shows itself in the attraction of a monistic or pantheistic solution to life. Whatever be the stimulus the problem of the one and the many calls for an answer, and it has evoked many answers. How can finite beings exist of themselves, and with all their imperfections, and coexist with what is infinitely perfect being? The simplest answer is to say that only the One really exists, and that the rest is either illusion or a moment in the circular or evolutionary movement of the One. This explanation tidies up the universe at whatever cost. If it is supported by the misery, the pangs and longings of human experience, the answer becomes more and more impressive. The final touch bringing conviction is the spiritual experience attained by techniques of self-denial and contemplation of what is and is not. As the self sheds its customary habits, its anxieties and private concerns, its thoughts and desires and passes into a great solitude, there comes over it a feeling beyond mind and beyond self, an experience as of being identified with the All. There is no proper way of describing it, and so some are content with negatives, while others use descriptive terms, such as the bliss of not being or absorption into the divine.

This is a form of gnosis, a gnosis hidden from the gross-minded and the profane. It is an answer which has appealed to many; it gives a picture of unity—but the unity is gained at a price. It means the renunciation of multiplicity; there is no room in the system for liberty, for persons or for a living God. In the descriptions, indeed, of this sophia the language changes at times from that of the loftiest abstractions to the personal. Sri Aurobindo writes of the divine Spirit and of the self as if despite their essential unity they could be apart enough to share love. Something is lacking, and a philosophy which could keep the high notes of this gnosis, conceive of a unity and nevertheless restore what is wanting, namely, the place, however humble, of the finite and the personal, such a philosophy would contain more abundantly the perennial wisdom. The crux is the self. The Gnostics say that it is a spark of divinity. They are ashamed of the body and man as he is. Conscience does indeed make us traitors to ourselves as well as cowards, and since it is the flesh and selfishness which have made human history so ugly at times, they relinquish the self and commit their all to the spirit. But human nature is not given over entirely to evil, nor are its doings without beauty. What Shakespeare called the "momentary grace of mortal men" is so precious that all the efforts of art are directed to perpetuating it. The soul and body are often at war, but they want each other, and we are most ourselves in adhering to our word of honor and to the promises of love in marriage, and in believing, almost against the evidence, in the unchanging value of virtue and truth. Our present anxieties have called out a new category to signalize what is in fact an age-long experience. This is the category of "Presence," so vividly delineated by writers like Louis Lavelle, Emil Brunner, Gabriel Marcel and Ralph Harper. Lavelle tells us that "the initial experience" of life is always "the experience of the presence of being," and Marcel that "presence is not conferred on being by the *I* but on the *I* by being." A human person cannot come to the proper consciousness of his identity without contact with others and nature. In giving names to what is alive around him he discovers his own name, and in the presence of others his longing to lose himself and to find himself is fulfilled. Without the love of others the two longings turn to egotism or self-abandonment. Now in the religious experience the soul meets what is infinitely removed from it and yet is present, and it is made aware both of the infinite grandeur of God and of the abyss which separates such a being from its own infinitesimal self. This initial experience should canonize the relations between God and the self, for in the light of it it would be the wildest blasphemy for the self to call itself divine. But while the divine is felt to be wholly other, it is not a presence which is tangible. It does not usually make an impact on the soul like to that of a thunderstorm or of a friend coming into the room. The soul is left in its loneliness with a nostalgia for its original experience. As it came forth from God—"Thee God I come from, to Thee go"—it craves for return, and so the cycle begins of withdrawal, of self-searching, of meditation and self-denial. In dying to self it begins to have a sense of deliverance, of belonging to something greater, and so the centrifugal movement grows stronger with fewer and fewer counterclaims from the centripetal. In the depths of the soul, where all external voices have been hushed, the very marks which served to keep the identity or the self are lost, and so high and ecstatic is the experience that it seems that there is nothing in between the ocean of divinity and itself. Only if there be a God *known* to be wholly other is the self left conscious of its own identity and finite condition, for this knowledge stays with the self and keeps the relation one of love between persons, between the "I and the Thou." Knowledge, though the mystics are tempted to despise it, plays a vital part in safeguarding mystical experience from illusion. The soul is carried away by what is happening to it, and forgets its birthright and all landmarks. In such a state it is nothing and it is all, as the language of the mystics, so prone to opposites, shows. Human knowledge is not at home on these heights, but it knows the slopes and the true direction, and so it serves the mystic as a seeing man guides the steps of a blind poet.

Many have fallen by the wayside, deceived by their interior lights and states; the authorities on the mystical life give warning of its dangers and traps, both in the East and in the West. Long experience has given the masters of the spiritual life in the East an empirical knowledge, amounting to a second sense, of how to behave in order to go forward. Aided by this they have dispensed with intellectual tests. In the West, however, there has been in the Catholic tradition the external test of right belief. Faith being an intellectual virtue governs spiritual experience, and therefore when the experience becomes mystical and above ordinary reason the intellect is not left behind; it is still active, making faith and experience coincide. St. Teresa of Avila bears testimony of this. She was not well educated and knew none of the intricacies of theology. At the time she lived there were at least three different spiritual movements by which she might easily have been unconsciously affected. A Neo-Platonist school taught that in the eternal Logos of God, an emanation of the divine Mind, could truth alone be found. The Illuminists were spreading the Gnostic belief that God was a universal essence of which man was part, and that in the despoiling of himself he would come to realize his unity with the Godhead. Servetus and Juan de Valdés— each in his own way, constructed a patchwork of Christian, Neo-Platonic and Arabian mystical elements. In the midst of these currents of thought St. Teresa remained, for a simple and untrained person, astonishingly sure-footed. She could in her early works even mistake the imagination for the understanding and fancy that the higher powers of the soul were in the top of the head. She was bafflled how to express herself, for "spiritual things are so difficult to express, especially to express clearly, above all those which take place only in the soul, that if obedience does not come to my help it is doubtful if I shall succeed." Nevertheless her highest and most interior experiences of union with the divine come to us in the language of love of the Christian Holy Trinity, and whereas the theologian often stammers inexactly about this most intricate of mysteries, Teresa is both articulate and right. The object of her faith is the object of her love, and having given herself wholly to God, she becomes the recipient of his truth; "the soul in this state is all golden, and on this motionless, docile gold, God spreads the preciously prepared enamel of His gifts."

In *Mother and Son* by I. Compton-Burnett one of the characters remarks: "You can do as you will with solitude. It does not take you on equal terms." The man who lives in a private world of his own ceases to know himself and becomes mad, in that he has no standard wherewith to judge himself. He is not taken "on equal terms." Those who are privileged to enjoy and suffer interior religious experiences of an exceptional order are open to the same danger. The affective state is so intense, what is happening is so out of the common, that the soul may be at a loss as to what it is and what it has become. In normal experience we are brought up against an external reality which takes our measure, and if we fool ourselves it punishes us. In its resistance to us it is both a cure and a stimulus, and our selfhood is confirmed and strengthened by it. When we care for another or fall in love, we become still more aware of ourselves and our failings, and at the same time we feel a thousand times more alive. But when the object is withdrawn, and the soul, all creatures abandoned, seeks its own best being within, it takes a great risk, for the solitude may not take it on equal terms. It is in the dark, in its own "artifice of eternity." If we had an intuition of our own substance and selfhood, all would be well, because we should then be able always to rely on a fixed point of reference and guide ourselves by it. But as most philosophers agree and experience shows, we have no such intuition. This is the reason why in the Christian tradition the practice is observed of testing spiritual and mystical experiences by external criteria, such as the structure of Christian belief and worship, the solidarity of love within the Church, and humility of spirit. What serves most convincingly for proof against self-deceit is the presence and at the same time the otherness of God. It is the conjunction of these two certainties in the account given by St. Teresa of herself which creates such an impression of sanity and wisdom. God is what so many would like to think God must be, and Teresa herself, despite her humility, so obviously grows in stature the more she loves and surrenders herself to God. The enamel is being added to "the motionless docile gold." Nothing is subtracted from the perfection of the divine being in the created beauty of such natures, and a philosophy which can preserve order within reality, the while it increases the dignity of human nature, improves upon the so-called perennial wisdom which metamorphoses that nature into the One.

"The only adequate cure for anonymity is the gift of presence." * The presence of another disturbs our reveries and our private world by bringing us back to reality and to an awareness of ourselves. God, from whom we come, to whom we go, is the commanding presence, the totally other in whom, nevertheless, "we live and have our being." He speaks to us in the Word and meets us in love. We are not left to our-

* Mr. Ralph Harper in *The Sleeping Beauty*, p. 127.

selves, to burrow into the arcana of the self; we have no need to rely upon techniques, however well tested, to keep in the path of truth. Inner experiences, like those of Pascal or the saints, may illumine the surrounding darkness, but where there is no dependence on truth otherwise known, they may be interpreted wrongly. There are so many unknown factors at work. Part of the experience, for all we know, may derive from our part-earthly origin and be a kind of exhalation from the common source of our bodies, that Mother Earth which has in the past excited such mystical adoration. There is, too, the underground of the self, that unconscious, whence, it is suggested, the great images and archetypes emerge and work magically on the mind. We have to reckon also with the play upon the mind of tradition and inheritance, of environment and all the contagious ideas and sentiments of a particular time. The anima, as the evidence shows only too well, grows restive under the yoke of reason, and when it runs wild it knows no bounds; it finds delirious excitement in irrationality, in Dionysiac frenzies and in a dance of death.

Philosophy begins in wonder and grows with knowledge, the knowledge of what is external, and the knowledge of the self and of God. The heights to which man can reach in religious experience have given a special dye to the meaning of wisdom in the Eastern philosophies; and in the West Christianity has separated off what it calls a supernatural wisdom. The modern school of perennial philosophy would amalgamate these two in a sophia, which contains the best of both. Halfway to the heights there is a wisdom which has, also, a habitation. The path to it is by true knowledge and true love, and these are not necessarily the outcomes of mystical techniques or of explorations into the dark places of the self. Knowledge is kept upright and face forward by interest in and respect for what is objective, and self-knowledge grows step by step with the discipline of the mind and the emotions, provided that the mind starts to grow on the proper soil. "I came like Water, and like Wind I go" is the conclusion of those who try to sow the seed of wisdom in an unfertile ground. Nature and the self both come from the same hand, and the first principle of a nourishing knowledge is certainty as to one's origin, status and destination. This certainly gives meaning to the need of self-purification and to the accumulation of learning, to the purgative and illuminative ways, which usually take time and experience and are marked by suffering. As the years pass the wise are more and more easily discerned; to them belong a candor and simplicity, a reverence for nature and for man, and a modesty of judgment and utterance. The knowledge they acquire is never cheap or venal; it is the fruit of devotion to truth and patience, and it is not a card index but a store in which the contents are gathered in their proper place and degree. In the amassing of knowledge affection plays its part— not as an interloper or as a partisan; it serves, rather, to bring the alien object closer to the mind, and it acts as a kind of engagement ring betokening fidelity to the work of the intellect and making thereby its insights more intimate. In human relations those especially are called wise who know what is in man, are not perturbed by his frailties or pretensions nor duped by popular estimates; they are neither sentimental nor cynical, and for that reason and because their judgments seem, like an old tree, to be a thousand-year-thick, their good advice is sought and their words treasured. Wisdom, then in short, as a lay and human attribute, belongs to a man, when, resting on the calm certainty of his origin and destiny, he is wide in his interests, can assess degrees of value in life, seeks with Aristotle for an intuitive apprehension of "those things which are most precious in their nature," and is like Job humble before mystery.

Beyond this there stretches a higher wisdom. In the Eastern philosophy it is attained when man sheds his larval state and becomes divine; in the Christian view it is the gift of grace. "I'll be wise hereafter, and seek for grace." St. Thomas Aquinas distinguishes not only between natural and graced wisdom, but also between the virtue and the gift. "The plenitude of knowledge gained by some through study and an acuteness of intellect is the virtue the Philosopher called wisdom. But in others a plenitude of knowledge is gained by an affinity to divine things as Denis wrote of Hierotheus, who learned divine things by experiencing them." The gift of wisdom and the virtue of it differ again because of the manner in which the highest truths are learned. To quote John of St. Thomas: "The gift of wisdom in a loving and mystical way attains divine things which are the supreme causes. This mystical experience is properly considered a gift of God. For although all the supernatural habits and virtues are gifts of God, it is one thing to attain to an object by means of a gift and quite another to attain to it because of the gift as if the act of giving with which God gives Himself to us pertained to the essence of the act of attaining the object. God gives Himself through His Spirit and His will, inasmuch as He opens His heart. The primary thing in any gift is that the giver should open his heart and give himself or his will to another. He should be joined to the other person in heart, i.e., in spirit and love, according to David: 'If you come peaceable to me . . . let my heart be joined to you.' " In this description of wisdom St. Thomas fuses knowledge and love and joins hands with St. Francis of Assisi and the Franciscan school, which sees love everywhere. "If I come forth by way of Sight, Love, Love is all around," as Jacopone Da Todi cries. Human thought, when it leaves the things of sense, becomes impersonal, and it is love which brings back distinctness. That is why love is the covenanted way of talking about the union between persons, whether of one person with another or of a finite person with God. In the love of persons nothing is lost, for love gives increase and does not take away. In the Christian philosophy "He Who is" lifts up what is always dependent on Him, and as nothing in comparison, into a quasi-equality of love. The human self is so graced that it can share the divine secrets and pass into union with God without any loss of its own being. The fire of love does not destroy; it enkindles and illumines. This means in terms of wisdom, that we are able in St. Paul's words, "to catch the glory of the Lord as in a mirror, with faces unveiled; and so we become transfigured in that likeness . . ."; or as Ruysbroeck describes it; there is a "a new birth and a new enlightenment without interruption; for the ground from which the Light shines forth, and which is the Light itself, is life-giving and fruitful, and therefore the manifestation of the Eternal Light is renewed without ceasing in the hiddenness of the spirit. . . . Behold, the delight and the joy which the Bridegroom brings with him in his coming are boundless and without measure, for they are himself. And the grasp of the spirit is opened so wide for the coming of the bridegroom, that the spirit itself becomes the Breadth which it grasps. And so God is grasped and beheld through God; wherein rests all our blessedness." The "breadth" of which Ruysbroeck writes is the attribute which conspicuously belongs to the wise man, whether secular or spiritual. The spiritually wise have become so identified by love with God that they "have the mind" of God, see with his eyes and have his regard for their fellow men. Those of us who live now are immensely beholden to the geniuses of the past. We stand upon their shoulders, and we interpret our experience through the knowledge which they have handed down. What Euclid taught and Plato and Copernicus and Newton is part of our mental makeup. Our sensibilities, too, and imagination have been molded by such men as Michelangelo and Shakespeare and John Sebastian Bach. We see new aspects of the world and draw its beauties together because we have been looking through their eyes. This power of assimilating ourselves to others' loves and outlooks has its analogy in what happens when God graces us with his presence. St. Augustine says that "faith, too, has its eyes," new eyes which have an innocence and freshness, as if the old world, so familiar to us, had just been created anew. And this new light like the sky, does no prejudice to what is there and is true.

> The glass blue days are those
> When every colour glows,
> Each shape and shadow shows
>
> . . . .
>
> Hued sunbeam will transmit
> Perfect, not alter it.*

* From "The Blessed Virgin Compared to the Air We Breathe" by Gerard Manley Hopkins. From *Poems,* published by Oxford University Press.

What happens in these first stages of spiritual wisdom is well described by M. Mouroux in *The Christian Experience.* "There is within us someone who speaks and acts first, a sovereign initiative demanding our response; the response is a magnificent act of freedom, but the freedom is grafted upon the sovereign initiative. This is the first form of the passivity. Every Christian experience thus begins, so to speak, as a *laisser faire,* in an original *pati divina,* an original act of consent to the activity of the Spirit. And in this passive acceptance is accomplished the mysterious fecundation of the human spirit—its creation as a pneuma—by the power of the Spirit."

In accepting this new "fecundation" and attraction the human individual grows into the likeness of the divine Lover and comes to see something of the mystery of the divine Providence and plan. The wisdom to which St. Paul and St. John the evangelist primarily refer is the understanding of the eternal life promised in the Gospel; but this knowledge spills over into an understanding in degree of the Logos and the secret intentions of creation. St. Augustine touched this wisdom at Ostia; St. Thomas Aquinas at the end of his short life was so overwhelmed by it that his writings seemed as straw. Those who stand far off from these saints are, nevertheless, granted a beginning of this vision, if they are humble and work out the truth in love. "Where there is no vision the people perish." There is a scattered wisdom throughout the world and there have been manifestations of it in all ages, "sages standing in God's holy fire as in the gold mosaic of the world." If the attempt of the new school of perennial wisdom to find a highest common factor in the religious philosophies of East and West is stillborn, that does not mean that God has not revealed himself in sundry places and in sundry times. The magi have always had a star to lead them, as have all those who submit themselves to wisdom and have preferred "her beyond kingdoms and thrones, and esteemed riches nothing in comparison of her; and loved her above health and beauty, and chose to have her instead of light; for her light cannot be put out."